I0014857

DevOps with Kubernetes

Non Programmer's Handbook

2 Manuscript Bundle

© Copyright 2018 - All rights reserved.

DevOps
WITH
KUBERNETES

Non-Programmer's Handbook

DEV OPS

STEPHEN FLEMING

2 Manuscript Bundle

Copyright © 2018 Stephen Fleming

All rights reserved.

© Copyright 2018 - All rights reserved.

This document is geared towards providing exact and reliable information in regards to the topic and issue covered. The publication is sold with the idea that the publisher is not required to render accounting, officially permitted, or otherwise, qualified services. If advice is necessary, legal or professional, a practiced individual in the profession should be ordered.

- From a Declaration of Principles which was accepted and approved equally by a Committee of the American Bar Association and a Committee of Publishers and Associations. In no way is it legal to reproduce, duplicate, or transmit any part of this document in either electronic means or in printed format. Recording of this publication is strictly prohibited and any storage of this document is not allowed unless with written permission from the publisher. All rights reserved.

The information provided herein is stated to be truthful and consistent, in that any liability, in terms of inattention or otherwise, by any usage or abuse of any policies, processes, or directions contained within is the solitary and utter responsibility of the recipient reader. Under no circumstances will any legal responsibility or blame be held against the publisher for any reparation, damages, or monetary loss due to the information herein, either directly or indirectly.

Respective authors own all copyrights not held by the publisher. The information herein is offered for informational purposes solely, and is universal as so. The presentation of the information is without contract or any type of guarantee assurance. The trademarks that are used are without any consent, and the publication of the trademark is without permission or backing by the trademark owner.

All trademarks and brands within this book are for clarifying purposes only and are the owned by the owners themselves, not affiliated with this document.

Contents

Book 2: Kubernetes Handbook

Book 1- DevOps Handbook

Introduction to DevOps and its impact on Business Ecosystem

BONUS DEVOPS BOOKLET

Dear Friend,

I am privileged to have you onboard. You have shown faith in me and I would like to reciprocate it by offering the maximum value with an amazing gift. I have been researching on the topic and have an excellent "DevOps Booklet" for you to take your own expedition on DevOps to next level.

- Do you want to know the job requirement of DevOps Engineer?
- Do you want to know statistics of DevOps job available and mean salary offered?
- What are the latest trends in DevOps methodology
- People to follow on the latest on DevOps development

Also, do you want once in a while updates on interesting implementation of latest Technology; especially those impacting lives of common people?

"Get Instant Access to Free Booklet and Future Updates"

- Link: http://eepurl.com/dge23r

- QR Code : You can download a QR code reader app on your mobile and open the link by scanning below:

1. Introduction

DevOps is the buzzword these days in both software and business circles. Why? Because it has revolutionized the way modern businesses do business and, in the process, achieved milestones that weren't possible before. And in this book, you'll learn what DevOps is, how it evolved, how your business can benefit from implementing it, and success stories of some of the world's biggest and most popular companies that have embraced DevOps as part of their business. It is my hope that by the time you're done reading this book, you'll have a good idea of how DevOps can help your business grow.

So if you're ready, turn the page and let's begin.

2. What is DevOps

DevOps – or development and operations – is a term used in enterprise software development that refers to a kind of agile relationship between information technologies (IT) operations and development. The primary objective of DevOps is to optimize this relationship through fostering better collaboration and communication between development and IT operations. In particular, it seeks to integrate and activate important modifications into an enterprise's production processes as well as to strictly monitor problems and issues as they occur so these can be addressed as soon as possible without having to disrupt other aspects of the enterprise's operations. By doing so, DevOps can help enterprises register faster turnaround times, increase frequency of deployment of crucial new software or programs, achieve faster average recovery times, increase success rate for newly released programs, and minimize the lead time needed in between modifications or fixes to programs.

DevOps is crucial for the success of any enterprise because, by nature, enterprises need to segregate business units as individually operating entities for a more efficient system of operations. However, part of such segregation is the tendency to tightly control and guard access to information, processes and management. And this can be a challenge, particularly for the IT operations unit that needs access to key information from all business units in order to provide the best IT service possible for the whole enterprise. Simply put, part of the challenge in segregating business units into individually operating ones that are independent of each other is the relatively slow flow of information to and from such units because of bureaucracy.

Moving towards an organizational culture based on DevOps – one where the enterprise's operations units and IT developers are considered as "partners" instead of unrelated units – is an effective way to break down the barriers between them. This is because an enterprise whose culture is based on DevOps is one that can help IT personnel provide organization with the best possible software with the least risk for glitches, hitches, or problems. Therefore, a DevOps-based organizational culture is one that can foster an environment where segregated business units can remain independent but, at the same time, work very well with others in order to optimize the organization's efficiency and productivity.

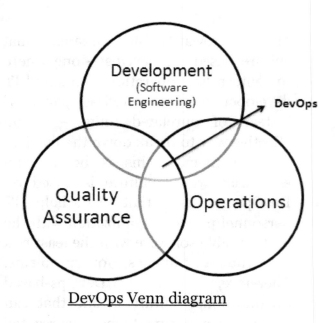

DevOps Venn diagram

Key Principles

One characteristic of DevOps is that it isn't grounded or dependent on stringent processes and methodologies. It's based more on key principles that allow an enterprise's key business units to efficiently work together and, in the process by breaking down any "walls" that may prevent optimal working relationships among such units. These key principles that guide an enterprise's DevOps are culture, measurement, automation and sharing.

Challenges Solved By DevOps

Just before the development of DevOps, it took several teams to collate the necessary data and informational requirements as well as writing code. After that, another team – a QA team – performed tests on new codes in a separate software development environment once the necessary requirements were met. Eventually, it's the same QA team that releases the new code for deployment by the enterprise's operations group. After that, the deployment teams are divided further into groups referred to as "silos" which include database and networking. And if you consider all the teams involved with the development and deployment of just one code, you won't be surprised why many enterprises suffer from project bottlenecks.

With such a set up, several undesirable things happen. One is that developers often become unaware of roadblocks for Operations and Quality Assurance that may keep the new programs from working as they were designed to work. Another thing that may happen is that as the QA and Operations teams work on so many features of the program, they may not have a true understanding of the purpose and value of the programs that are being developed/tested, which may keep such teams from effectively doing their work on such programs. Lastly, inefficiency and unnecessary backlogs are highly probable given each team or group has their own goals and objectives to achieve, which often times oppose those of the other groups, as well as the tendency to absolve themselves of responsibility for things that go wrong.

With DevOps, these potential problems can be addressed via creation of cross-functional teams that collaborate and share a common responsibility for maintaining the systems that are responsible for running software and other programs, as well as for prepping up the software so that they run on said systems with excellent feedback mechanisms for possible automation issues.

A Typical Scenario That Illustrates the Need for DevOps

Imagine that an enterprise's development team (the Dev team) releases a new program "over the wall" to Quality Assurance – the QA team. At this point, the QA team assumes the responsibility of discovering as many errors as possible in the new program, if any. Without any good working relationship – or any relationship at all for that matter – chances are high that the Dev team will be very defensive about the errors found by the QA team on their newly developed program, especially if there are lots of them. At which point, it's highly possible for the Dev team to even blame the QA team for such errors or bugs in the program. Of course, the QA team will deny that it's them or their testing environment that's to blame for the errors or bugs and that at the end of the day they're just there to discover bugs that exist within the programs developers create. In other words, the QA team will just revert the blame for the errors back to the Dev team. It can become nasty.

Let's say, after several attempts, the bugs and errors were fixed and the program has fully satisfied the QA team. They now release the program to the operations team concerned, a.k.a., the Ops team. But the Ops team refuses to fully implement the new program because they feel that too much change too soon will hamper their ability to do their jobs effectively. So they limit their system's changes. As a result, their operating system crashes and blames the Dev team for it, notwithstanding the fact that their refusal to implement the system fully led to the crash.

Defending their honor and glory, the Dev team blames the Ops team for not using the program the way it is designed to be used. The blaming continues on for a while until finally, someone has the sense to intervene and eventually lead the teams to cooperate their way into fixing the program. But the delay and the losses were already incurred.

The Continuum

One very practical way to look at the various DevOps aspects is to use what's called the **DevOps continuum**. The vertical axis represents the 3 delivery chain levels of DevOps, which are continuous integration (lowest level), continuous delivery, and continuous deployment (highest level). The bottom horizontal plane or axis represents people's perceptions of what DevOps is focused on, where the left side represents an automation or tools perspective while the right side represents a culture perspective. Others feel strongly that DevOps must be focused more on culture than tools while for others, it's the other way around.

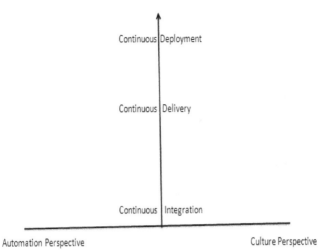

Continuous Deployment

Continuous Delivery

Continuous Integration

Automation Perspective   Culture Perspective

DevOps Continuum

The ideal location is the upper right hand corner, i.e., continuous deployment under a cultural perspective. Organizations that are located at this part of the continuum are considered as endangered species or unicorns simply because they're few and far in between. **Very good examples of these "unicorns" include Etsy,**

Netflix, Flicker, Amazon, Google and Pinterest.

Bloggers, coaches and some thought leaders usually paint a DevOps picture that's located on the upper right corner of the continuum. They may also have a strong bias towards either tools or culture. While it's not necessarily bad to have robust debates or discussions as to which is more important (tools or culture), the fact remains that organizations need both in order to optimize their productivity. Culture won't be productive without the necessary tools and tools won't work properly without the support of a very good culture.

It's important for organization to realize that moving up to the DevOps Nirvana spot in the continuum takes time. Many times, the first move is to combine tools, culture and continuous integration, which is at the lower wrung of the continuum. It shouldn't be an issue because DevOps isn't a very simple and easy activity and as such, it takes many baby steps and some time to maximize.

An optimal DevOps may be different for each organization because it's a blend of tools, culture, and maturity, all of which should make sense. And those that make sense is often relative and can change over time. What's crucial here is are continuous efforts to minimize – or even eliminate – any obstacles or bottlenecks for each software delivery phase through improvements in the automation processes and collaboration between silos or business units.

DevOps Maturity Phases

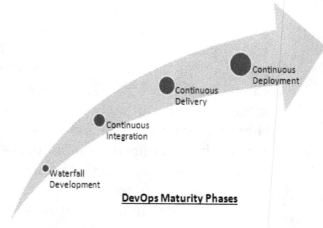

DevOps Maturity Phases

In order to keep track of an organization's DevOps progress, it's important to be cognizant of the maturity phases involved in DevOps. These include:

Waterfall Development: Prior to continuous integration, development teams write a ton of code for several months. When they're done with

22

writing code, the teams will then combine their finished codes together so that they can release it. The code will come with different iterations or versions that are so different from each other and would probably undergo quite a number of changes that its integration process may take several months to complete. As such, this process may be considered as an unproductive one.

Continuous Integration: This refers to the quick integration of newly developed code with the existing main code body that will be released. This phase can help the team save a ton of time, especially when they're ready to release the code already.

This phase or process wasn't conceptualized by DevOps. Continuous integration is a practice that originated from the Extreme Programming methodology, which is an integral part of an engineering process called Agile. While it's been around for quite a while, this process or term was adopted by DevOps because every successful execution of continuous integration requires automation. As you learned in the DevOps continuum, continuous integration is the first level of the DevOps maturity phase. This involves checking codes in, collecting it into a binary executable code in most cases, and doing basic testing to validate the code.

Continuous Delivery: This phase may be considered as an extension of the previous one and is stage 2 of the DevOps stage. During execution of this DevOps phase, adding extra automation and testing is needed in order to make newly developed codes ready for immediate deployment with practically no human intervention whatsoever. This is a good way to augment an organization's need to be able to frequently merge newly developed codes with main code lines. At this phase, an organization's code base is in a constant state of ready deployment.

Continuous Deployment: This shouldn't be confused with the previous phase, continuous delivery. This is considered to be the most advanced DevOps phase and is a condition wherein organizations are able to deploy programs or codes directly to production without the need for any kind of human assistance. As such, it's considered to be the "nirvana" of DevOps and this makes companies "unicorns."

Teams that make use of continuous delivery never deploy codes that aren't tested. Instead, they run new codes through a series of automated testing procedures prior to pushing them to the production line. Typically, only a small percentage of users get to receive newly released codes where an automated feedback system is used to monitor usage and quality of the code prior to full release.

As mentioned earlier, only a few companies are already in this phase – the **nirvana phase** – of DevOps because doing so takes time and serious resources. But given that most organizations find continuous integration quite a lofty goal, many often aim for continuous delivery instead.

The Focus of DevOps

Establishing a culture of collaboration and using automation (with DevOps tools) as a means to improve an organization's efficiency are the main focus of DevOps. While there's a tendency to be biased towards either tools or culture, the truth is it takes some combination of both tools and culture for an organization to become optimally productive.

Culture

When talking about culture within the context of DevOps, the point of focus is on increasing collaboration, reducing isolation of units (silos), sharing the responsibilities, increasing each team's autonomy, increasing quality, putting a premium on feedback and raising the level of automation. Most of what DevOps values are the same as those of the Agile system because it's an extension of the latter. We'll talk more about Agile later on but in a nutshell, Agile may be considered as a holistic software delivery system that measures progress through working software. Under Agile, developers, product owners, UX people, and testers all work as a tight-knit unit to achieve a common goal.

As an extension of the Agile system, DevOps involves adding an operations' mindset – and possibly a team member with some

operational responsibilities – to the team. In the past, the progress of DevOps was measured in terms of working software. These days, it's measured in terms of working software that's already in the hands of the end users or customers. This is achieved only through shared system (runs the software) maintenance responsibilities, close collaboration via breaking down of silos or obstacles to such collaboration and preparation of the software so that it'll run in the system with high delivery automation and quality feedback.

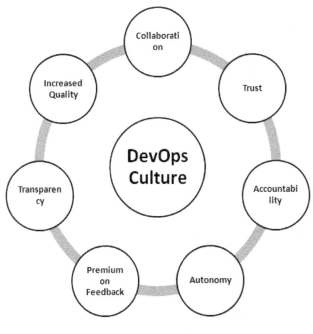

DevOps Culture

Tools

When talking about DevOps tools, we talk about configuration management, building and testing of systems, deployment of applications, control over different versions of the program or code, and tools for monitoring quality and progress. Each of the maturity phases of DevOps – continuous integration, delivery, and deployment – all need a different set of tools. While it's true that there are tools commonly used in all the phases, the number and kinds of tools needed increase as an organization moves up through the chain of delivery.

And speaking of tools, some of the most important ones include:

Source Code Repository: This refers to a place where codes are checked in and changed by developers. The repository manages the different iterations of code that are checked in it, making it possible for developers to avoid working on each other's works. Some of the most popular tools used as code repository include **TFS, Bitbucket, Cloudforce, Subversion and Grit.**

Build Server: This refers to an automation tool that collects code in the source code repository into an executable code base. Some of the most popular tools include **Artifactory, SonarQube, and Jenkins.**

Configuration Management: This defines how an environment or a server is configured. Popular tools include **Chef and Puppet**.

Virtual Infrastructure: This type of infrastructure lets organizations create new machines using configuration management tools like **Chef and Puppet**. These infrastructures are provided by cloud-vending companies that sell platform as a service (PaaS) or infrastructure and include Microsoft's Azure and Amazon Web Services. Organizations can also get "private clouds", which are private virtual infrastructures that allow fur running a cloud on top of the hardware in an organization's data center. An example of this is **vCloud by VMware.**

When combined with automation tools, virtual infrastructures can help empower organizations that use DevOps to configure their servers with no need for human intervention. An organization can test brand new codes simply by sending them to their cloud infrastructure, creating the necessary environment, and running all necessary tests with no need for any human fingers to touch a computer's keyboards.

Test Automation: When doing DevOps testing, the focus is on automated testing to make sure that only fully deployable or working codes are deployed to production. Without an extensive automated testing strategy, it's hard – if not downright impossible – to achieve a state of continuous delivery with no human intervention where organizations can be confident about the codes they deploy into production.

Some of the most popular tools for test automation include **Water and Selenium**.

Pipeline Orchestration: Think of a pipeline as a factory assembly line. Further, think of this as the time when the development team finishes writing the code until the code is fully deployed in production.

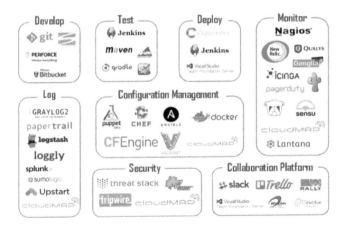

Source of above image: emaze.com

DevOps Tools Landscape

34

3. The DevOps Evolution

Many organizations have experienced much success when it comes to using Agile methods for hastening the delivery of software. Starting from the development organization, Agile has slowly increased its scope to include other important areas like operations and information technology (IT). Teams and sub-teams have learned how to streamline processes, improve the quality of feedback mechanisms and how to speed up the innovation processes in IT departments. All of these have had significant effects on organizations' productivity.

To capitalize on these developments, continuous delivery and DevOps were created with the aim of connecting organizations' development teams with IT operations primarily via automated systems. By doing so, organizations were able to foster an environment of increased the responsiveness, agility and faster software delivery times to the market.

Back in 2001, a document called **The Agile Manifesto** emerged from the software development environment and introduced what is now called as Agile Development. Methodologies based on the Agile system oriented software developers in the art of breaking down the software development process into much smaller bites that are called "user stories". These "stories" helped speed up feedback acquisition processes, which in turn helped organizations align their products' features with the needs of their markets much faster.

Agile focused on helping small teams and developers work much more efficiently and smarter. At first, only small software startup companies who were excited to disrupt what was then the current software market and who were willing to do that through trial and error were into the Agile system. As the process gradually evolved and matured, the whole software community started to become more and more responsive and accepting of methodologies based on the Agile system.

In turn, such increasing acceptance made the concept of "scale" more and more important in the industry. Developers were able to come out with functioning programs or software codes much faster. But when it come to the downstream processes of testing and deployment of newly developed codes, two things prevented organizations from increasing the turnaround or delivery times of quality software to their intended users: fragmented processes and the existence of functional silos, i.e., segregated operating business units.

Eventually, the Agile system gave birth to new technologies and processes that were aimed at automating and streamlining the whole cycle of software delivery. With the coming of age of continuous integration or CI, smaller and more frequent code releases became the norm as more and more codes needed to be tested and integrated daily. This in turn put a huge strain on Quality Assurance (QA) and Operations (Ops) teams.

A breakthrough book by Jez Humble titled Continuous Delivery helped promote the idea that the entire software lifecycle can be viewed as one automatable process. It was so effective in promoting said idea that even Fortune 1000 companies started embracing this idea. In turn, the perceived value of Agile initiatives that were at the time blocked and stalled and in the process, also helped increase the stakes for treating software delivery as a crucial and strategic initiative in business.

Agile focused on the needs of code developers. On the other hand, continuous delivery and DevOps initiatives helped organizations become much more efficient, productive, and profitable. These two have also helped organizations improve their software delivery cycles.

Many industry experts believe that DevOps and CD – as Agile system extensions – have the biggest chance for organizations to optimize their enterprise values. An industry expert once said about CD that if the software delivery cycle is a concert, Agile is the opening act and CD is the show's main performer.

Software-driven organizations that continue to evolve in terms of technical frameworks and processes have already transitioned from just implementing continuous integration to continuous delivery. In doing so, CD has transformed software delivery as we know it and has extended the potential of Agile by linking DevOps practices and tools with CI or continuous integration.

Continuous delivery is – from a technical viewpoint – a collection of methodologies and practices that are focused on improving software delivery processes and optimize the reliability of organizations' software releases. It makes use of automation – from continuous integration builds all the way to deployment of codes – and involves all aspects of research and development and operations organization. At the end, CD helps organizations release quality software systematically, repeatedly and more frequently to their end users or customers.

Leading software expert Martin Fowler developed key tenets for Agile-based continuous delivery, based on successful agile methodologies. He outlined key questions to ask in continuous delivery such as:

- Can the organization readily deploy your software through its entire lifecycle?
- Can the organization keep the software deployable and prioritize it even while working on its new features?
- Is it possible for anyone to receive quick and automated feedback about their applications and infrastructures' production readiness whenever a person modifies or changes them?
- Is it possible for the organization to just push a button to deploy any version of software whenever it's needed?

Extending the Agile system through continuous delivery provides organizations several benefits including:
- A faster time to deploy software to the market;
- Better quality of products;
- Higher customer satisfaction;

- Higher productivity and efficiency;
- Increased reliability for software releases; and
- The capability to create the right products.

Agile's impact in the software industry has been both highly disruptive and far-reaching. It has also helped promote new ideas outside of itself, which includes multi-functional processes (DevOps) as well as continuous delivery (CD) that impact both software end users and organizations. With the onset of DevOps and CD, waterfall approaches have been archived in the annals of software history and communication and collaboration continue to remain important aspects of an organization's operations.

Timeline

For a better understanding of the evolution of DevOps and CD, here's a timeline of crucial events in their development.

A software development consultant by the name of Patrick Debois tried to learn all of IT's aspects. Within 15 years, Patrick has assumed quite a number of different roles in the Information Technology sector so that he can work in just about every role imaginable within an IT organization, the goal of which was to get a holistic yet intimate understanding of Information Technology. Developer, system administrator, network specialist, project manager, and tester – you name it and Patrick Debois has worked it.

In 2007, Patrick took on a consulting job for a huge data migration center organization and was in charge of testing. That meant he spent a huge chunk of his time working with development and operations (DevOps).

43

For the longest time, Patrick had been uneasy about how differently Devs and Ops worked. In particular, he became frustrated with the way work was managed between these two groups when it came to data migration.

That time, CI or continuous integration was starting to become very popular within the Agile circle and was brining development ever so closer to deployment. Still, there was a void when it came to bridging the huge gap between Dev and Ops. At this point, Debois had a strong sense of sureness that there has got to be a much better way for these two particular groups to work much better.

2008

Patrick chanced upon a post at the 2008 Agile Conference by Andrew Shafer, wherein the idea for a session that'll discuss an agile infrastructure. After seeing the post, Patrick attended the session but unfortunately, the idea was very badly received to the point that only Patrick showed up. Not even Andrew Shafer, the brains behind the idea, bothered to show up at the session he himself called for!

But that didn't stop or discouraged Patrick Debois. With his enthusiasm over knowing he wasn't alone with his ideas or point of view concerning the divide between Dev and Ops exceeding that of a kid in a candy store, he ultimately tracked Andrew Shafer down and formed a Google group named Agile System Administration.

2009

Flickr's Senior VP for Technical Operations John Allspaw and Director For Engineering Paul Hammond presented "10 + Deploys Per Day: Dev and Ops Cooperation At Flickr" at the 2009 O'Reilly Velocity Conference in San Jose. This presentation provided what will ultimately become the groundwork for improving software deployment via improvements in the way Dev and Ops work together.

Though Patrick was in Belgium at the time of the presentation, he was able to catch it via live streaming. This presentation encouraged him to come up with his own conference in Ghent, Belgium: DevsOpsDays. This conference was able to gather together a very lively group of futuristic thinkers who are passionate about how to improve software development. Even more important is that the group maintained and publicized the conversation over Twitter using #DevOpsDays as its hashtag. In an attempt to optimize Twitter's limited character limit, the group eventually truncated the hashtag into #DevOps.

2010

46

In 2010, the DevOpsDays conferences were held in the United States and Australia. The conference was conducted in more countries and cities all over the world over time. And this fostered even more face-to-face meeting between like minded IT people, which in turn made more IT people excited about the idea of DevOps until it came to a point that DevOps became a full-fledged grassroots movement.

2011

Prior to 2011, the grassroots movement known as DevOps was primarily driven by open source tools and individuals with hardly any attention from software vendors and analysts. But on that year, DevOps started infiltrating the mainstream by getting the attention of top analysts such as Jay Lyman and Cameron Haight from 451 Research and Gartner, respectively. As a result, the big boys of the software industry started to take notice and even market DevOps.

2012

DevOps – at this time – was fast becoming a buzzword in the industry. As a result, the DevOpsDays conference continued with its growth all over the world.

2013

By this time, several authors have begun writing books on DevOps as a result of the growing insatiable public thirst for information related to DevOps. Some of these authors include Mary and Tom Poppendiek with Implementing Lean Software Development, and Gene Kim, Kevin Behr and George Spafford with The Phoenix Project.

2014

Some of the world's biggest companies started to incorporate DevOps into their

organization.   These   include   Lego,
Nordstrom and Target.

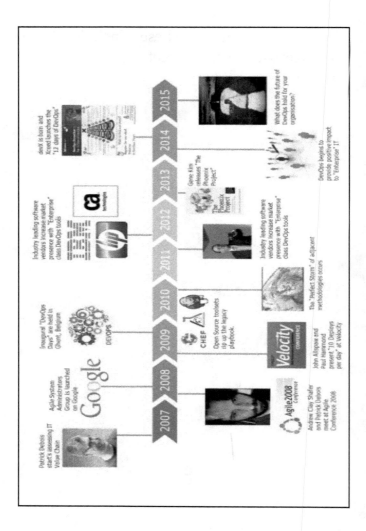

Source: Article "Evolution of DevOps" on LinkedIn

4. The Agile System and DevOps/CD

From out of the need to keep up with the increasing speed at which software is developed and the increasing number of software being developed and released as a result of such increasing speed, which Agile methods have allowed organizations to achieve, came forth the DevOps. It may be considered as the love child of Agile software development, as significant advancements in methods and culture through the years have brought to fore the need for an approach to the entire software delivery cycle that's more holistic.

What Is The Agile System?

The Agile system or Agile Development is a general word used to refer to numerous incremental and iterative software development methodologies. Among these methodologies, the most popular ones **are Extreme Programming (XP), Lean Development, Scaled Agile Framework (SAF), Kanban, and Scrum.**

Despite each methodology having their own unique approach, all of them have common threads – vision and core values. All of them basically incorporate continuous feedback and iteration for successfully refining and eventually, delivering a software system. All of them also involve continuous planning, testing, integration, and other kinds of continuous evolution both in terms of the software and the projects. All of them are also lightweight compared to other old-school approaches or processes such as Waterfall-type ones. Also, these methodologies are naturally adaptable. But the most important commonality among these Agile methods is the ability to empower people to quickly and effectively collaborate and make decisions together.

At first, developers made up most Agile teams. As these teams started to become more and more efficient and effective in producing software, it became obvious that having separate development (Dev) and quality assurance (QA) teams was an inefficient way of doing things. As a result, Agile methodologies started to encompass the QA process so that the speed at which software is delivered can be much faster. Agile continues to grow, which now includes delivery and support members, so that Agile can encompass all aspects from ideation to delivery of software.

The ideals of DevOps are able to extend the development practices of Agile through the rationalization of how software moves through all stages – building, validating, deployment, and delivery. It does so while empowering cross-functional units or teams by giving them complete ownership of the software application process from design through production support.

DevOps and Agile

Essentially, DevOps is simply the expansion of principles used by Agile. It includes systems and operations and doesn't just stop dealing with concerns once codes are checked in. Aside from collaborating as a cross-functional unit made up of developers, testers, and designers that comprise an Agile team, DevOps also includes operations people in its cross-functional units. This is because instead of just focusing on coming up with a software that works, which is what Agile's all about, DevOps aims to provide customers with a complete service, i.e., a working software that's effectively and efficiently delivered to its end users or customers. DevOps emphasizes the need to minimize or even eliminate obstacles and barriers to effective collaboration between software developers and operations (end users), making the most out of their combined skills.

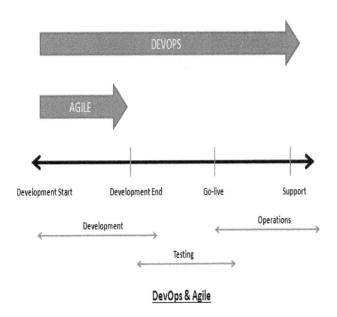

DevOps & Agile

While Agile teams make use of automated building, automation testing, continuous integration and continuous

55

delivery, DevOps extends Agile teams a bit more to include "infrastructure as code", metrics, monitoring, configuration management and a tool chain perspective to cloud computing, virtualization, and tooling in order to speed up changes inside the world of modern infrastructure. Also, DevOps incorporates other tools like orchestration (e.g., zookeeper, mesos, and noah), configuration management (e.g., cfengine, ansible, chef, and puppet), containerization, virtualization and monitoring (e.g., docker, vagrant, OpenStack and AWS), and many others.

As you can see, DevOps is merely an extension of the Agile system that encompasses operations in its definition of cross-functional Agile teams and fosters collaboration between developers and operations in order to fully deliver working software to their end users.

5. Scrum

Scrum refers to an Agile methodology or framework for managing projects that's primarily used for projects involving software development, the goals of which are to deliver new software features or capabilities every other week or month. Scrum is one approach that heavily influenced the document known as the Agile Manifesto that enunciates a particular set of principles and values that help guide organizations make decisions related to the faster development of high-quality software.

The use of Scrum has already encompassed other business activities such as marketing and information technology, where projects need to move along in complex and ambiguous environments. Many leadership teams also use Scrum as their Agile management method, usually mixing it with Kanban and lean practices.

Scrum and Agile

Scrum may be considered as a sub-type of the Agile software development system. Agile, if you may recall, is comprised of principles and values that describe an organization's daily activities and interactions. In and by itself, Agile is neither specific nor prescriptive.

Scrum adheres to Agile's principles and values but also includes further specifications and definitions. In particular, these additions pertain to specific practices concerning the development of software. And while Scrum was developed for Agile software development, it has become a preferred framework by which Agile projects in general are managed. Occasionally, Scrum is also called Scrum development or Scrum project management.

Some of the benefits of using Scrum include:
- Better satisfaction among stakeholders;
- Faster time to market;
- Happier members or employees;
- Higher quality products;
- Improved dynamics between teams and members; and
- Increased productivity.

This methodology can address work complexities by among other things, more transparent data or information. Through improved transparency, the organization's stakeholders can check and if necessary, adjust or adapt depending on the current or actual condition or environment the organization's in instead of projected conditions or environments. This ability to check and adjust lets organizations or teams to work on many of the common shortcomings of waterfall development processes, which include among others:

- Confusion as a result of frequently changing requirements;
- Inaccurate reporting of progress;
- Software quality compromises; and
- Underestimating of costs, resources, and time.

In Scrum software development, transparency in common standards and terms is a must so that delivered software meets expectations. Inspecting frequently helps to ensure continuous progress and help the organization detect any unwanted variations in results early enough to enable quick and timely adjustments. When it comes to inspection and adaptation, the most popular Scrum events include Sprint Planning, Stand Ups (a.k.a., daily Scrum), Sprint Retrospective and Sprint Review.

Scrum Components

The Scrum Agile development methodology is made up of key components: team roles, ceremonies (events), artifacts, and rules. Normally, scrum teams are made up of 5 to 9 members with no specific team leader who decides how to attack a specific problem or who delegates project tasks. Decision-making is a collegial process, i.e., the whole team – as a unit – gets to make decisions regarding solutions to problems and issues faced by the team. Every Scrum team member plays an essential part in coming up with solutions to problems faced by the team and is anticipated to bring a product all the way from conception to finalization.

In Scrum teams, members can take on 3 roles, namely that of a product owner, Scrum master, and the development team. A product owner is a project's primary stakeholder. Normally, a product owner is an external or internal customer, or a customer's representative. There can only be one product owner and he or she determines or communicates the project's overall mission and vision that the team is expected to build or develop. Ultimately, the product owner's accountable for taking care of product backlogs and accepting finished work increments.

The ScrumMaster role is assigned to a person who will serve as the product owner, development team, and organization's servant leader. The ScrumMaster acts more like a facilitator considering the lack of hierarchical authority over development teams, and ensures the team's adherence to Scrum rules, practices, and theories. He or she also protects the development team by doing everything he or she can to assist the team in optimizing its performance. "Everything" may include things like helping the product owner manage backlogs, facilitate meetings and remove obstacles or impediments.

The Development Team is a cross-functional unit that's self-organizing and is equipped with all the necessary skills for delivering shippable increments every time a sprint or iteration is completed. Under the Scrum methodology, the role "developer" expands to include the role of any person involved in the process of creating the content for delivery. For members of the development team, there are no titles and there's no one who tells the team how to convert backlog items into increments that can already be shipped to customers.

Ceremonies (Scrum Events)

A sprint refers to a time-boxed period in which particular types of work are finished and are prepared for review. Normally, sprints last for 2 to 4 weeks but it's not impossible to hear of sprints that conclude within 1 week only.

Sprint planning refers to team meetings that are also time-bound or boxed. These help determine which among a product's backlog items will be shipped to the end user and how to actually do it.

Daily Stand Ups refer to very short meetings not exceeding 15 minutes. In said meetings, each member of the team covers progress made in the project since the last stand up in a fast and transparent manner, any obstacles that are hindering him or her from progressing in the project and any work planned prior to the next meeting.

Sprint reviews refer to events where in the development team gets the opportunity to demonstrate or present completed work during sprints. Here, the product owner checks the work vs. pre-determined criterion for acceptance and based on such criterion, approves or rejects the finished work. Here, the clients and stakeholders also provide valuable feedback that ensures each and every increment delivered is up to the customer's needs and specifications.

Retro – a.k.a. the retrospective – refers to the final team meeting during the sprint to find out the things that went well, those that went bad, and how the development team can further improve its performance in succeeding sprints. This meeting's attended by the team members and the ScrumMaster and is a crucial opportunity for the team to set its sights on improving overall performance and determine continuous improvement strategies for its processes.

Artifacts or Documents

Scrum artifacts include product backlogs, sprint backlogs, and increments. A product backlog is possibly the most valuable Scrum document or artifact, which lists every product, project, or system requirement.

65

The product backlog may be viewed as a list of things to do, where each item on the list is equated with a deliverable that provides business value. These items are ordered or ranked according to their business value by the product owner.

A sprint backlog refers to a list of items sourced from the product backlog. In particular, these items are those that need to be completed in a sprint or iteration.

Increments are the sum of all product backlogs that have already been addressed or completed from the time the latest software version was released. The product owner decides when to release increments but it's the team's responsibility to ensure everything that comes with an increment is ready for release. These ready-for-release items are also referred to as Potentially Shippable Increments or PSIs.

Scrum Rules

66

When it comes to rules that govern Scrum, they're entirely up to the team and should be determined by what is best for their particular processes. The most competent Agile coaches will instruct teams to begin with some of the most basic Scrum events discussed earlier and then review and adapt according the team's particular needs. Doing so ensures continuous improvements in how teams collaborate.

6. Kanban

Kanban is a way of managing the product creation process. It emphasizes continuous delivery (CD) without having to overburden an organization's development (Dev) team. It's also designed to improve collaboration between an organization's different units. Kanban is based on 3 key principles:

- Visualization of the things done today, i.e., the workflow. The ability to see everything within the context of each other can provide a lot of useful information to the organization.
- Limiting the amount of work-in-progress (WIP), this helps bring balance to a flow-based approach that helps an organization's teams avoid taking on too much work all at once.
- Flow enhancement, i.e., as soon as a task is done, work is started

on the next highest order task from the backlog queue.

Consistent with DevOps and CD, Kanban helps promote ongoing collaborations and promotes active and continuous learning and improvement by defining an optimal team workflow. And for any DevOps initiative, the implicit goals are fast movement, rapid deployment, and responsiveness to a rapidly changing business environment. Kanban – as a methodology – is a very helpful and progressive tool for achieving an organization's desired outcome. In particular, the ability to be able to monitor an organization's progress and status on a daily basis instead of weekly isn't just a very appealing proposition but one that can also transform the way an organization is able to communicate and complete its tasks.

The Kanban approach or methodology helps developers work as one solid unit and finish everything they've started. If through the Kanban principle on limited Work-In-Progress a part of the development team is obligated to allocate their resources into other aspects of an ongoing project to assist in its completion, these members will be able to see the project from a larger and different perspective. This can be helpful in identifying possible issues, obstacles and bottlenecks even before they manifest and cause problems.

The ability to see projects from a holistic point of view by as much of its stakeholders as possible helps teams and the organization to adapt a system-level view. Within the underpinning principles of DevOps, this is referred to as the first way, the outcomes of which include:

- Known defects are never passed to downstream work centers;
- Local optimizations are never allowed to create global degradation;

- Continuous seeking of increased work flow;
- Continuous seeking of deeper and more profound understanding of the system; and
- Removal of the "time box" out of the equation.

Using a Kanban approach to the DevOps movement is one that requires nerves of steel because it's relatively new compared to its other Agile brothers, particularly Scrum. As such, there's much discussion about how it's more appropriate for initiatives that are time-critical like a change management endeavor or a product launch that's happening in 7 days' time. Regardless, the Kanban methodology is still one that's worth taking into consideration and checking to determine potentially beneficial changes that it may bring to an organization, specifically to its workflow. More importantly, the Kanban methodology can help an organization determine whether or not it's close to violating acceptable WIP limits. But the biggest gains that can be enjoyed from using Kanban is in finding an organization's work process constraints.

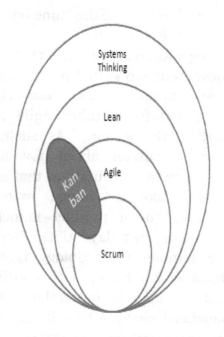

Agile Scrum & Kanban

7. Kanban versus Scrum

With Scrum, product owners only have a limited amount of time to incorporate user stories into a sprint, which is between 2 to 3 weeks. This however poses a problem – unusual breaking points are created for people who deploy and test the software. Too little stories may not result in shippable products towards the end of an iteration or sprint, may increase dependence between sprints or iterations, and may lead to very challenging coordination efforts and very difficult testing.

Using the Kanban approach on the other hand, frees up product owners from any time limitations. This is because the Kanban methodology is all about focusing on the most significant work and getting them done through processes to the right people and at the right times.

To get a better idea of the differences between the Scrum and Kanban Agile methodologies, let's take a look at two of its most crucial differences: rules and workflow.

Rules

Both the Scrum and Kanban software development methods have rules governing the performance of work. The Scrum method is the more prescriptive of the two. There are 23 mandatory and 12 optional rules for Scrum implementation per Agile Advice, which include:
- Daily meetings must be held;
- During iterations or sprints, no interruptions are allowed;
- Product owners should create and manage a backlog of its products;

- Progress should be measured using a burn-down chart;
- Teams must be cross-functional; and
- Time for work is boxed.

Collectively, such rules make for quite a rigid system in which teams must work to successfully implement Scrum in their software development. There are 2 major challenges to this. One is called ScrumBut, i.e., organizations use "Scrum, but..." This means many organizations – due to the methodology's rigidity – tend to ignore some of the methodologies rules, which leads to a non-optimal use of the Scrum framework.

The other challenge presented here is the time box, which are great for distraction-less working time for software developers to deliver specific products, and providing regular bases for stakeholders by which to steer and evaluate projects. But looking at it from the lenses of DevOps, workflow is regularly broken by specific software delivery checkpoints or milestones. Such disruption in workflow makes it challenging for organizations to coordinate sprint dependencies and ensure successful transfer of software from development to production.

When you evaluate the Kanban software development methodology, you'll find that it's substantially less restrictive. Consider it only has 2 rules, which are:
- Workflow visualization; and
- Setting limits to amount of work-in-progress.

Yep – that's all folks! Having only 2 rules, this methodology is a very open and flexible one, which can be easily utilized under any environment. In some organizations, Kanban is even used outside of software development, from product manufacturing to marketing! You can even incorporate some of Scrum's work rules into Kanban if you so desire. That's how flexible it is.

Because Kanban focuses more on the workflow instead of time boxes, it's the better choice for utilizing with DevOps. Because Kanban emphasizes the optimization of the whole software delivery process instead of just the development phase, many software development experts think it's the perfect "spouse" for DevOps.

Workflow

The other major difference between Kanban and Scrum is the workflow. This particular difference is an offshoot of the difference in its rules. With Scrum, you choose the features that need to completed in the next sprint beforehand. Afterwards, the sprint or iteration is "locked," the work is performed over the sprint's duration (usually in a couple of weeks), and at the sprint's end, the cue is vacant or empty.

By locking the sprint in, the work team is assured of ample and necessary time for working on a problem without any interruptions from other seemingly urgent requirements. At the end of each iteration or sprint, feedback sessions help stakeholders approve or disapprove work that's already been delivered and steer the project depending on changes in the organization's activities or environment.

When using the Kanban methodology for developing software, an organization isn't subject to sprint time constraints. Instead, the much focus is given on ensuring that workflow remains uninterrupted and without any known issues as it moves downstream.

Limits, however, are placed on the amount of work queued or in progress under the Kanban methodology. It means that at any given point time in the software delivery cycle, the team can only work on a certain number of issues or features. In setting such a limit, teams are compelled to focus on only a few work items on hand, which often leads to high quality work.

A visible workflow fosters a sense of urgency for teams to keep things moving. Keep in mind that the Kanban methodology was a product of manufacturing genius and as such, its focus is on efficiency and productivity. And as it's extended to the software development arena, it incorporates important aspects of software development success like participation of stakeholders.

DevOps, Kanban, and Scrum

For organizations use DevOps, increased efficiencies, more frequent deployment of features, and high responsiveness to business demands are some of their most important goals. As such, each of the two methods can help organizations address various areas of their DevOps better than the other. While Kanban seems to be all the rage these days, it's not necessarily the automatic choice for organizations.

If an organization is responsible for developing new features that need stakeholder feedback and high developer focus, then Scrum is possibly the better choice for its DevOps. In this scenario, Scrum's sprint lock feature and demos for stakeholders at the end of each sprint or iteration can be very, very valuable to the organization.

If an organization is accountable for simple maintenance and is more reactive than the regular organization, Kanban may be the better option. This is because it has greater flexibility in terms of responding to stakeholder feedback and it doesn't require locking of backlogs.

At the end of the day, every organization's different and as such, they should know their teams' strengths and areas for improvements in order to choose the best software development method. At some point, it may even be optimal to get the best of both methodologies and combine them into one for the optimal achievement of an organization's goals.

8. Organizational Culture Change For DevOps Success

DevOps started as a method for developing software, which was intended to hasten the software building, testing, and release processes by making two crucial teams – Operations (Ops) and Developers (Dev) – collaborate more effectively. In effect, this has to do with organizational culture.

But how exactly does organizational culture play a big role in successful employment of DevOps in organizations, particularly within tech organizations? Lucas Welch of Chef explains this by giving his working definition of DevOps, which is a professional and cultural movement that focuses on how high velocity organizations are built and operated, which is derived from its practitioner's personal experiences. He explains further that tech companies need to provide their employees a safe enough environment, enough freedom, and access to knowledge when needed if they want to succeed in a DevOps environment. Further, he explains that its team members must be empowered to think, speak, and ask without restraint or hindrance in order for them to quickly act. When done correctly, this type of collaboration among teams helps empower and engage team members with a purpose, aligned leadership, and shared sets of beliefs and values.

However, it's easier to talk about the integration of 2 teams with totally different subcultures than to actually integrate them. Based on a research done by Gartner, out of the 75% of IT departments that would've tried to come up with a bi-modal capacity by the year 2018, only less than 50% will enjoy the benefits that come along with using new software development techniques like DevOps. And according to Gartner's Research Director Ian Head, up to 90% of I&O organizations that try to use DevOps without first addressing their particular cultural foundations will eventually fail.

DevOps discussions appear to be about some new concept and methodology, but they have been circulating in the industry for long now. It's just that such concepts have gone around using different names.

But this doesn't do anything to reduce the value of the DevOps movement. Tech companies have started to get that focusing on improving collaboration between businesses units that seem to lie on opposite poles of the organization can lead to increased productivity and product quality.

Often times, the challenge in changing an organization's culture to suit DevOps are shifting the focus from the technical side of DevOps to the cultural aspect of it. It has been realized across board that organizational culture change is the most important factor for maximizing improvements from adapting this methodology.

Things to Consider

In order to successfully change an organization's culture for optimization of DevOps benefits, the following should be considered:

Dialogue Space: An organization must be able to provide a space or venue where all parties involved in DevOps can meet and talk. It shouldn't be a surprise to find that when people are asked to change the way they operate in terms of performing their functions within the organization, they'd feel anxious and resistant – at least in the beginning. An organization can help provide a very good foundation for transitions like these by giving members who'll be affected by the implementation of DevOps opportunities to interface with one another in an environment that's safe and secure so that they can fully grasp the need for DevOps implementation. The organization can also ensure proper clarification of roles, responsibilities, and interdependencies to help affected members feel secure and at peace with the implementation of DevOps because often times, ignorance is the source of anxieties and insecurities.

Leader Support. An organization's leaders are some of the key stakeholders when it comes to transitioning into DevOps and as such, it must be able to provide the necessary support for them – i.e., tools, abilities, skills, and knowledge – that will enable them to lead other members through a successful transition to DevOps. Sadly, many organizations make the fatal mistake of assuming that their leaders already know what to do and have all the necessary skill sets for the job at hand. Organizations only realize such mistakes during transition, when leaders are unable to successfully lead their teams and in the process, hamper the entire transition process.

Stakeholder Engagement: In certain ways, DevOps needs key groups or teams in the organization to change their current perspectives, assumptions, and beliefs concerning how to best get their works done. By getting these groups or teams involved in the process of redefining their work along the lines of DevOps, organizations can help make them see that they are important parts of the change to be implemented instead of feeling that the organization is doing something nasty to them.

Accept Mistakes: When an organization asks their key people – most if not all of whom already have deeply-entrenched career identities – to change the way they see and think about collaborating with others to achieve a new common goal, hiccups are bound to happen despite the best laid plans and preparations to avoid them. Simply put, mistakes will happen along the way and what's more important and realistic is for an organization's leadership to react properly towards these situations because this will affect how people involved in the DevOps transition will move forward. If leaders immediately use punishment as a means of rectifying mistakes and hopefully preventing their recurrence, there's a high risk that team members will go back to their familiar place of safety – their old ways of doing things. If the organization's leaders can use mistake moments as opportunities for teaching members the proper way of doing DevOps and learn to live with such mistakes as a normal part of doing something new, the organization will be able to rebound from hiccups and glitches much faster and achieve full DevOps implementation at the soonest possible time.

Cynicism Vs. Skepticism: Skepticism in light of being presented with crucial new information about how to best get work done is normal. Consider the fact that when people have been doing their work for so many years with hardly any changes, certain key beliefs and assumptions of how to do their jobs and how to collaborate with others in the performance of their jobs become as hard as cement. So when DevOps is initially presented to them, it's ok for them to be skeptical about it. But over time, their minds will gradually change as they see the great benefits of implementing DevOps. But cynicism is an altogether different beast. While the minds of skeptics are open to the possibility of being convinced otherwise, cynics are hard set on what they think and believe to be true and as a result, they normally reject all claims contrary or not in line with their current belief systems. If skeptics believe in "guilty until proven innocent", cynics believe "immediately guilty regardless of evidences to the contrary that may be presented later on...period!" Organizations will be better off identifying the cynics in their teams and excluding them from DevOps transition and full implementation when possible.

Time: Everything worth doing successfully takes time. The only difference is how much time is needed. It's the same with organizations that are transitioning to DevOps and embedding it as part of an organization's new culture. As team members start to see more and more of DevOps benefits as time goes by, the more they'll naturally be aligned to its principles and practices. At a certain point in time, DevOps will become a natural part of an organization's culture. A fatal mistake would be to expect DevOps to be fully integrated and ingrained in an organization's culture very quickly. Doing so will lead to frustration and drastic corrective measures that can sabotage efforts instead of maximizing them.

A Holistic Approach

At the very center, DevOps is all about collaboration and teamwork. And that can only happen when people's hearts and minds are generally – not perfectly – in sync. That is the power of culture and when an organization is able to successfully foster a culture of collaboration and openness to change, then successful transition to and implementation of DevOps is not far behind.

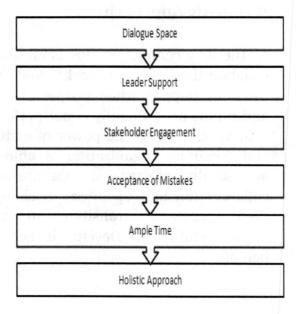

Factors for Organizational Change to adopt DevOps

92

9. DevOps Ecosystem and emerging trends

Refer the below line:

"Only 10% of companies describe themselves as fully digital." – **Datum**

Any organization, big technology firm or a small e-commerce firm, all are aiming to be fully digital. While there is a major focus on the disruptive technologies which would lead the next digital wave; the modus operandi of its execution is equally important. The true Digital Transformation can be achieved by creating DevOps culture and environment.

The DevOps Environment

DevOps is an environment, not a technology. Designing, Developing, Deploying, and Operating in a unified environment is the key aspect of DevOps

93

methodology. Continuous deployment and integration facilitates the faster rate of software development, testing and operations. Efficiency and automation are the major pillars of this methodology.

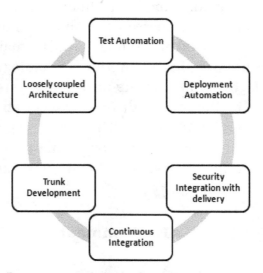

<u>Factors creating positive DevOps Environment</u>

To explain it further,

Automation

Automation allows the high performers
of the system to focus more on
innovation rather than operational
activities. One example could be cited of
transformation at HP LaserJet. On the
way to transformation, the organization
followed continuous delivery practice
and invested in automation (major focus
on automated testing). This resulted in
multiple fold increase in time invested
in developing new features or
innovation.

Trunk Development

A model, where developers' works on
software code in a single branch called
'trunk' and they resist creating other
long standing development branches by
practicing techniques. They avoid any

merger step and do not break the continuity.

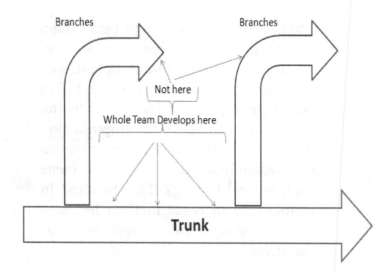

Practically, developers work in small high performing teams and develop off the trunk (on branches). The pragmatic way for best delivery performance could be:

- Daily merger of code into trunk.
- Branches with day log or less lifetimes

- Three or less active branches.

DevOps Architecture (Loosely Coupled)

Continuous delivery is driven greatly by the team and architecture which are loosely coupled. Loosely coupled team can complete their tasks independently. Similarly, loosely coupled architecture is the one where any modification can be done in the individual component or service without making changes in the dependent services or components.

The loosely coupled architecture results in strong IT and organizational performance because the delivery team can perform testing and deployment without depending on other teams for any work or approvals. It also avoids back- and – forth communication, making the process smooth and efficient.

97

Overall, it can be stated that more than automation of test and deployment process; the flexibility provided by loosely coupled architecture contributes towards continuous delivery.

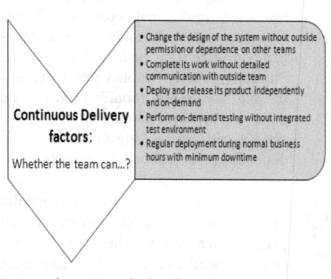

Continuous Delivery factors:

Whether the team can...?

- Change the design of the system without outside permission or dependence on other teams
- Complete its work without detailed communication with outside team
- Deploy and release its product independently and on-demand
- Perform on-demand testing without integrated test environment
- Regular deployment during normal business hours with minimum downtime

Emerging Trends in DevOps

1. **Containers and Micro services would be integrated**

big time with DevOps: "One of the major factors impacting DevOps is the shift towards micro services," says Arvind Soni, VP of product at Netsil

✓ **Microservices:** It is a application development architecture where applications are developed independently and are deployable, modular and small. Also, each modular service runs unique process and communicates in a defined manner serving business goals.

✓ **Containers:** It is an operating system virtualization method that facilitates application to run in resource isolated process. So, the application is deployed quickly, reliably and consistently in any deployment environment.

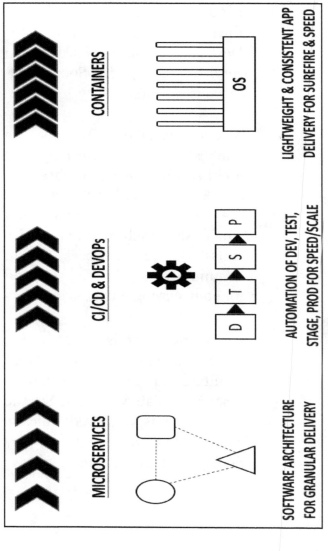

MICROSERVICES   CI/CD & DEVOPs   CONTAINERS

OS

D → T → S → P

SOFTWARE ARCHITECTURE
FOR GRANULAR DELIVERY

AUTOMATION OF DEV, TEST,
STAGE, PROD FOR SPEED/SCALE

LIGHTWEIGHT & CONSISTENT APP
DELIVERY FOR SUREFIRE & SPEED

2. **Expert teams practicing DevOps would cut down on security nets**: It may be the case that expert DevOps teams may decide to no longer have pre-production environment. The team may be confident and the process of deploying and testing in staging environment may be avoided. Again this may be the case with expert teams who are confident to **identify, monitor** and resolve issues on production.

3. **Spread and integration of DevOps:** More frequent usage of the term "DevSecOps," reflects the intentional and much early inclusion of security aspect in the software development lifecycle. DevOps is also expected to expand into areas such as database teams, QA, and even outside of IT also.

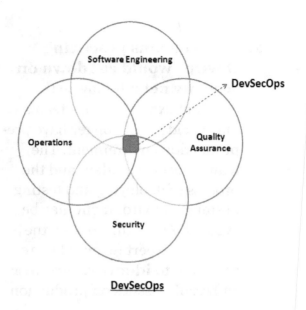

DevSecOps

4. **Increase in ROI**: As we move ahead in the DevOps way of application development IT teams would be more efficient and methodologies, processes, containers and micro services would contribute into higher ROI."The Holy Grail was to be moving faster, accomplishing more and becoming flexible. As these components find broader

adoption and organizations become more vested in their application the results shall appear," says Eric Schabell, global technology evangelist director, Red Hat.

5. **Evolution of success metrics:** On the path to DevOps evolution few points regarding the performance measurement matrices have been realized:
   ✓ Too many metrics to be avoided
   ✓ DevOps metrics should point out what's most important to you
   ✓ Business outcome relationship of the metrics are the key to standardization

Few of the DevOps metrics that may be relevant for the organization may be:

   ✓ Customer ticket volume
   ✓ % of successful deployment
   ✓ Job satisfaction of the deployment team

- ✓ % increase in time for innovation or adding new features

Overall, it is expected that all stakeholder would come together including security and database teams. The frictions caused by these teams would propel the number of releases exponentially.

10. DevOps Success Stories

Amazon is probably the most recognizable DevOps success story because simply put, it's one of the biggest and most recognizable companies in the world. Prior to implementing DevOps, Amazon was still running on dedicated servers. That practice made it very challenging to predict the amount of equipment they need to procure just to be able to meet website traffic demands. In an effort to minimize risks of being unable to meet those demands, Amazon had to pad their equipment requirement estimates just to have leeway for unusual or unexpected spikes in website traffic, which led to excess server capacity, i.e., server capacity wastage of up to 40%. And during shopping seasons like Christmas, up to 75% of server capacity was left unutilized. Economically, that was a very bad proposition.

Amazon's DevOps journey started when it transitioned to the AWS or Amazon Web Services Cloud. This allowed Amazon's engineers to incrementally scale capacity up or down as the need arose and let to substantial reductions in server capacity expenses. It also allowed Amazon to continuously deploy code – DevOps nirvana – to servers that needed new code whenever they want to.

Within 12 months from moving to AWS, Amazon's engineers were able to deploy code every 12 seconds or less on average. By switching to an Agile approach, Amazon was able to bring down significantly both the frequency and duration of website outages, which in turn increased its revenues.

Another very popular DevOps success story is **Wal-Mart** – the undisputed king of American big-box retail. While it's the undisputed king in physical shopping, it always lagged and struggled behind Amazon. In an effort to cut

Amazon's lead and gain much needed online ground, the company put together a very good team by acquiring several tech firms en route to establishing its own technology and innovation arm in 2011, WalmartLabs.

Through WalmartLabs, the parent company purposefully took a DevOps approach to establishing a powerful online presence. The technology and innovation subsidiary incorporated a cloud-based technology called OneOps, which automated and hastened the deployment of apps. Also, it came up with a couple of open source tools like Hapi, which is a Node.js framework that's used to build services and apps that in turn allowed the company's software developers to putting much of their effort and attention on programming multiple-use application logic. In turn, such application logic reduced the amount of time needed for building infrastructure.

By implementing DevOps, Wal-Mart was able to follow in the heels of Amazon.com and has substantially increased its revenues by foraging into the online market segment.

The most popular company that has successfully implemented DevOps is **Facebook.** The social media site practically changed the way the software industry thought about software development. Much of the initial principles it subscribed to in the beginning – including continuous improvements, automation, incremental changes, and code ownership – were considered to be DevOps by nature. Over the years, Facebook's approach has evolved, which has hastened its development lifecycle. In turn, the faster cycle continues to change the way people think about software. By being able to continuously deliver new updates to its app, Facebook continues to make people's experience in the social media platform even more fun, entertaining, and even addictive. It just gets better and better. And in doing so, Facebook was able to grow its business by leaps and bounds to the point where it became one of the biggest publicly listed companies in the New York Stock Exchange, the world's biggest stock market by capitalization. Below are the few latest examples of successful DevOps implementation:

Capital One's DevOps Success: Capital One is one of the largest digital bank in the world and it has been around for 20 years now. Capital One made a shift by adopting DevOps methodology to cater to growing requirements of Digital Banking Services. The approach changed when the engineers instead of writing codes for software and handing it to production team for testing ,fixing and pushing it to production worked together to complete the process using micro services and containers. They utilized the AWS cloud for running applications so that the IT team could focus on building digital products of highest quality.

Their team also insists the inclusion of databases in the DevOps adoption framework. This adoption makes databases respond much quickly to any change and saves time and provides return on investment.

American Airlines DevOps Success: After the acquisition of US Airways in 2013, the two IT teams decided to adopt DevOps as their answer their integration and roadmap issues. It became an opportunity to drive a cultural change at the organization. The two teams working in tandem led to creation of new applications and improved coordinated working culture.

Adobe's DevOps Success: When the organization moved from packaged software to cloud model, it was required to make series of small software updates rather than traditional annual releases. This led to adoption of DevOps methodology to meet the required pace of automating and managing the deployments. This move resulted in better and faster delivery and product management.

Netflix DevOps Success: Since Netflix entered into uncharted territory of streamlining videos instead of shipping DVD's, it required disruptive technologies to sustain its business. Today, the rate at which Netflix has adopted and implemented new technologies through DevOps approach is setting new bars in IT.

Major Success Stories

11. Conclusion

Thank you for buying this book. I hope that through this, you've become familiar with DevOps and Continuous Delivery and how they can help you grow your business. But as the saying goes, knowing is only half the battle and, in this case, the battle for growing your business. The other half is action. As such, I highly recommend that you act on the general knowledge you've gained about DevOps and CD through this book by reading more advanced material on the topic.

I would really appreciate if you can leave your review/feedback on Amazon.

Here's to DevOps and Continuous Delivery for your business success my friend. Cheers!

Stephen Fleming

My Other Books available across the platforms in e-book, paperback and audible versions:

1. Blockchain Technology : Introduction to Blockchain Technology and its impact on Business Ecosystem

2. Love Yourself: 21 day plan for learning "Self-Love" to cultivate self-worth ,self-belief, self-confidence & happiness

LOVE YOURSELF

21 day plan for learning "Self Love" to cultivate self-worth, self-belief, self-confidence & happiness

STEPHEN FLEMING

3. Intermittent Fasting: 7 effective techniques of Intermittent Fasting

❖ **DevOps Handbook:
Introduction to DevOps
and its impact on
Business Ecosystem**

Here Is a Preview of what you'll learn...

- What is DevOps

- Relationship between Agile,
  Scrum, Kanban and DevOps

- DevOps Adoption: Organizational cultural Change

- DevOps Ecosystem

- Emerging Trends

- DevOps success stories

In the **<u>Bonus Booklet</u>** you will find out:

- ✓ DevOps Job Market overview
- ✓ Insights into DevOps job application
- ✓ People to follow on social media for updated news/development

- ✓

** If you prefer audible versions of these books, I have few free coupons, drop me a mail at: valueadd2life@gmail.com. If available, I would mail you the same.

Book 2: Kubernetes Handbook

A Non-Programmer's Guide

© Copyright 2018 - All rights reserved.

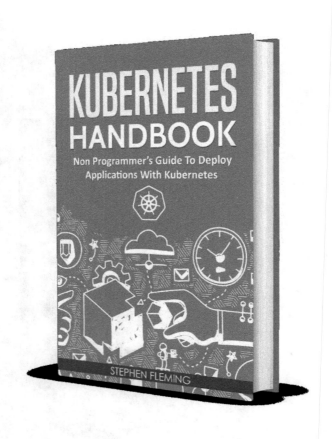

Copyright © 2018 Stephen Fleming

All rights reserved.

© Copyright 2018 - All rights reserved.

This document is geared towards providing exact and reliable information in regards to the topic and issue covered. The publication is sold with the idea that the publisher is not required to render accounting, officially permitted, or otherwise, qualified services. If advice is necessary, legal or professional, a practiced individual in the profession should be ordered.

- From a Declaration of Principles which was accepted and approved equally by a Committee of the American Bar Association and a Committee of Publishers and Associations. In no way is it legal to reproduce, duplicate, or transmit any part of this document in either electronic means or in printed format. Recording of this publication is strictly prohibited and any storage of this document is not allowed unless with written permission from the publisher. All rights reserved.

The information provided herein is stated to be truthful and consistent, in that any liability, in terms of inattention or otherwise, by any usage or abuse of any policies, processes, or directions contained within is the solitary and utter responsibility of the recipient reader. Under no circumstances will any legal responsibility or blame be held against the publisher for any reparation, damages, or monetary loss due to the information herein, either directly or indirectly.

Respective authors own all copyrights not held by the publisher. The information herein is offered for informational purposes solely, and is universal as so. The presentation of the information is without contract or any type of guarantee assurance. The trademarks that are used are without any consent, and the publication of the trademark is without permission or backing by the trademark owner.

All trademarks and brands within this book are for clarifying purposes only and are the owned by the owners themselves, not affiliated with this document.

Contents

BONUS TECHNOLOGY BOOKLET

Dear Friend,
I am privileged to have you onboard. You have shown faith in me and I would like to reciprocate it by offering the maximum value with an amazing booklet which contains latest technology updates on DevOps and Blockchain.

"Get Instant Access to Free Booklet and Future Updates"

- Link: http://eepurl.com/dge23r

OR

- QR Code : You can download a QR code reader app on your mobile and open the link:

Preface

This book has been well written as a guide to ***getting started with Kubernetes, how they operate and how they are deployed***.

The book also explains the features and functions of Kubernetes and how it can be integrated into a total operational strategy for any project.

Additionally, the reader will be able to learn how to deploy real-world applications with Kubernetes.

The book has been written in a simple, easy to comprehend language and can be used by Non-Programmers, Project Managers, Business Consultants or any other persons with an interest in Kubernetes.

1. Introduction

Kubernetes Defined

Kubernetes, also known as K8s is an open-source container-orchestration system that can be used for programming deployment, scaling, and management of containerized applications. Kubernetes were innovated with the aim of providing a way of automatically deploying, scaling and running operations of container applications across a wide range of hosts. A container is a standalone, lightweight and executable package of a part of the software that is composed of components required to run it, i.e., system tools, code, runtime, system libraries, and settings. Containers function to segregate software from its adjacentenvironment, i.e., for instance, variances in development and staging environments thereby enabling the reduction of conflicts arising when teams run separate software on the same network infrastructure.

Containers may be flexible and really

fast, attributed to their lightweight feature, but they are prone to one problem: they have a short lifespan and are fragile. To overcome this enormous problem and increase the stability of the whole system, developers utilize Kubernetes to schedule and orchestrate container systems instead of constructing each small component, making up a container system bullet-proof. With Kubernetes, a container is easily altered and re-deployed when misbehaving or not functioning as required.

Kubernetes Background

The initial development of Kubernetes can be attributed to engineers working in industries facing analogous scaling problems. They started experimenting with smaller units of deployment utilizing cgroups and kernel namespaces to develop a process of individual deployment. With time, they developed containers which faced limitations, such that they were fragile, leading to a short lifetime; therefore, Google came up with an innovation calling it Kubernetes, a Greek name meaning "pilot" or "helmsman" in an effort aimed at sharing their own infrastructure and technology advantage with the community at large. The earliest founders were Joe Beda, Brendan Burns and Craig McLuckie who were later joined by Tim Hockin and Brian Grant from Google. In mid-2014, Google announced the development of Kubernetes based on its Borg System, unveiling a wheel with seven spokes as its logo which each wheel spoke representing a nod to the project's code name. Google released Kubernetes v1.0, the first version of their development on July 21, 2015, announcing that they had partnered with Linux Foundation to launch the Cloud Native Computing Foundation (CNCF) to promote further innovation and development of the Kubernetes. Currently, Kubernetes provides organizations with a way of effectively dealing with some of the main management and operational concerns faced in almost all organizations worldwide, by offering a solution for administration and managing several containers deployed at scale, eliminating the practice of just working with Docker on a manually-configured host.

Advantages Of KUBERNETES

While Kubernetes was innovated to offer an efficient way of working with containers on Google systems, it has a wider range of functionalities and can be used essentially by anyone regardless of whether they are using the Google Compute Engine on Android devices. They offer a wide range of advantages, with one of them being the combination of various tools for container deployments, such as orchestration, services discovery and load balancing. Kubernetes promotes interaction between developers, providing a platform for an exchange of ideas for the development of better versions. Additionally, Kubernetes enables the easy discovery of bugs in containers due to its beta version.

2. How Kubernetes Operates

Kubernetes design features a set of components referred to as primitives which jointly function to provide a mechanism of deploying, maintaining and scaling applications. The components are loosely coupled with the ability to be extensible to meet a variety of workloads. Extensibility is attributed to the Kubernetes API, which is utilized by internal components coupled with extensions and containers that operates on Kubernetes. In simple, understandable terms, Kubernetes is basically an object store interacting with various codes. Each object has three main components: the metadata, a specification and a current status that can be observed; therefore, a user is required to provide metadata with a specification describing the anticipated state of the objects. Kubernetes will then function to implement the request by reporting on the progress under the status key of the object.

The Kubernetes architecture is composed of various pieces which work together as an interconnected package. Each component at play has a specified role, some of which are discussed below. Additionally, some components are placed in the container/cloud space.

- **Master**- It is the overall managing component which runs one or more minions.

- **Minion** –Operatesunder the master to accomplish the delegated task.

- **Pod**- A piece of application responsible for running a minion. It is also the basic unit of manipulation in Kubernetes.

- **Replication Controller**- Tasked with confirming that the requested number of pods are running on minions every time.

- **_Label_**- Refers to a key used by the Replication Controller for service discovery.

- **_Kubecfg_**- A command line used to configure tools.

- **_Service_**- Denotes an endpoint providing load balancing across a replicated group of pods.

With these components, Kubernetes operate by generating a master which discloses the Kubernetes API, in turn, allowing a user to request the accomplishment of a certain task. The master then issues containers to perform the requested task. Apart from running a Docker, each node is responsible for running the Kubelet service whose main function is to operate the container manifest and proxy service. Each of the components is discussed in detail in this chapter.

Docker and Kubernetes

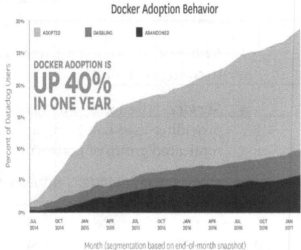

Docker Adoption Behavior

Month (segmentation based on end-of-month snapshot)

Source: Datadog

While Docker and Kubernetes may appear similar and help users run applications within containers, they are very different and operate at different layers of the stack, and can even be used together. A Docker is an open source package of tools that help you "Build, Ship, and Run" any app anywhere, and also enables you to develop and create software with containers. The use of a Docker involves the creation of a particular file known as a Dockerfile

134

which defines a build process and produces a Docker image when the build process is integrated to the 'Docker build' command. Additionally, Docker offers a cloud-based repository known as the Docker Hub which can be used to store and allocate the created container images. Think of it like GitHub for Docker Images. One limitation involved in the use of Docker is that a lot of work is involved in running multiple containers across multiple devices when using microservices. For instance, the process involves running the right containers at the right time; therefore, you have to work out how the containers will communicate with each other, figure out storage deliberations and handle or redeploy failed containers or hardware. All this work could be a nightmare, especially when you are doing it manually; therefore, the need for Kubernetes.

Unlike Docker, Kubernetes is an open-source container orchestration platform which allows lots of containers to harmoniously function together automatically, rather than integrating every container separately across multiple machines, thus cutting down the operational cost involved. Kubernetes has a wide range of functions, some of which are outlined below:

- Integrating containers across different machines.

- Redeploying containers on different machines in case of system failure.

- Scaling up or down based on demand changes by adding or removing containers.

- They are essential in maintaining the consistent storage of multiple instances of an application.

- Important for distributing load between containers.

As much as Kubernetes is known for container management, Docker also can manage containers using its own native container management tool known as Docker Swarm, which enables you to independently deploy containers as Swarms which then interact as a single unit. It is worth noting that Kubernetes interacts only with the Docker engine itself and never with Docker Swarm.

As mentioned above, Kubernetes can be integrated with the Docker engine with an intention of co-ordinating the development and execution of Docker containers on Kubelet. In this type of integration, the Docker engine is tasked with running the actual container image built by running 'Docker build.' Kubernetes, additionally, handles higher level concepts, including service-discovery, load balancing, and network policies.

Interestingly, as much as Docker and Kubernetes are essentially different from their core, they can be used concurrently to efficiently develop modern cloud architecture by facilitating the management and deployment of containers in the distributed architecture.

Containers are the new packaging format because they're efficient and portable

- App Engine supports Docker containers as a custom runtime
- Google Container Registry: private container image hosting on GCS with various CI/CD integrations
- Compute Engine supports containers, including managed instance groups with Docker containers

- The most powerful choice is a container **orchestrator**

Pods: Running Containers in Kubernetes

Pods area group of containers and volumes which share the same resource - usually an IP address or a filesystem, therefore allowing them to be scheduled together. Basically, a pod denotes one or more containers that can be controlled as a single application. A pod can be described as the most basic unit of an application that can be used directly with Kubernetes and consists of

138

containers that function in close association by sharing a lifecycle and should always be scheduled on the same node. Coupled containers condensed in a pod are managed completely as a single unit and share various components such as the environment, volumes and IP space.

Generally, pods are made into two classes of containers: a main container which functions to achieve the specified purpose of the workload and some helper containers which can optionally be used to accomplish closely-related tasks. Pods are tightly tied to the main application, however, some applications may benefit by being run and managed in their containers. For instance, a pod may consist of one container running the primary application server and a helper container extracting files to the shared file system, making an external repository detect the changes. Therefore, on the pod level, horizontal scaling is generally discouraged as there are other higher level tolls best suited for the task.

It is important to note that Kubernetes schedules and orchestrates functionalities at the pod level rather than the container level; therefore, containers running in the same pod have to be managed together in a concept known as the shared fate which is key in the underpinning of any clustering system. Also, note that pods lack durability since the master scheduler may expel a pod from its host by deleting the pod and creating a new copy or bringing in a new node.

Kubernetes assigns pods a shared IP enabling them to communicate with each other through a component called a localhost address, contrary to Docker configuration where each pod is assigned a specific IP address.

Users are advised against managing pods by themselves as they do not offer some key features needed in an application, such as advanced lifecycle management and scaling. Users are instead invigorated to work with advanced level objects which use pods or work with pod templates as base components to implement additional functionality.

Replication and Other Controllers

Before we discuss replication controllers and other controllers, it is important to understand Kubernetes replication and its uses. To begin with, being a container management tool, Kubernetes was intended to orchestrate multiple containers and replication. Replication refers to creating multiple versions of an application or container for various reasons, including enhancing reliability, load balancing, and scaling. Replication is necessary for various situations, such as in microservices-based applications to provide specific functionality, to implement native cloud applications and to develop mobile applications. Replication controllers, replica sets, and deployments are the forms of replications and are discussed below:

Replication Controller

A replication controller is an object that describes a pod template and regulates controls to outline identical replicas of a pod horizontally by increasing or decreasing the number of running copies. A Replication controller provides an easier way of distributing load across the containers and increasing availability natively within Kubernetes. This controller knows how to develop new pods using a pod template that closely takes after a pod definition which is rooted in the replication controller configuration.

The replication controller is tasked to ensure that the number of pods deployed in a cluster equals the number of pods in its configuration. Thus, in case of failure in a pod or an underlying host, the controller will create new pods to replace the failed pods. Additionally, a change in the number of replicas in the controller's configuration, the controller will either initiate or kill containers to match the anticipated number. Replication controllers are also tasked to carry out rolling updates to roll over a package of pods to develop a new version, thus minimizing the impact felt due to application unavailability.

Replication Sets

Replication sets are an advancement of replication controller design with greater flexibility with how the controller establishes the pods requiring management. Replication sets have a greater enhanced replica selection capability; however, they cannot perform rolling updates in addition to cycling backends to a new version. Therefore, replication sets can be used instead of higher level units which provide similar functionalities.

Just like pods, replication controllers and replication sets cannot be worked on directly as they lack some of the fine-grained lifecycle management only found in more complex tools.

Deployments

Deployments are meant to replace replication controls and are built with

143

replication sets as the building blocks. Deployments offer a solution to problems associated with the implementation of rolling updates. Deployments are advanced tools designed to simplify the lifecycle of replicated pods. It is easy to modify replication by changing the configuration which will automatically adjust the replica sets, manage transitions between different versions of the same application, and optionally store records of events and reverse capabilities automatically. With these great features, it is certain that deployment will be the most common type of replication tool used in Kubernetes.

Master and Nodes

Initially, minions were called nodes, but their names have since been changed back to minions. In a collection of networked machines common in data centers, one machine hosts the working machines. The working machines are known as nodes. The master machine is responsible for running special co-ordinating software that schedules containers on the nodes. A collection of masters and nodes are known as clusters. Masters and nodes are defined by the software component they run. The master is tasked to run three main items:

- API Server - The API server ensures that all the components on the master and nodes achieve their respective tasks by making API calls.

- Etcd - This is a service responsible for keeping and replicating the current configuration and run the state of the cluster. It is implemented as a lightweight distributed key-value store.

- Scheduler and Controller Manager- These processes schedule containers, specifically pods, onto target nodes. Additionally, they may correct numbers of the running processes.

A node usually carries out three important processes, which are discussed below:

- Kubelet- It is an advanced background process (daemon) that runs on each node and functions to respond to commands from the master to create, destroy and monitor containers on that host.

- Proxy - It is a simple network proxy that can be used to separate the IP address of a target container from the name of the services it provides.

- cAdvisor- It is an optional special daemon that collects, aggregates, processes, and exports information about running containers. The information may exclude information on resource isolation, historical usage, and key network statistics.

The main difference between a master and a node is based on the set of the process being undertaken.

The 10,000-foot view

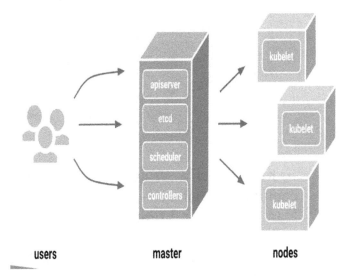

users   master   nodes

Services

A service assigns a fixed IP to your pod replicas and allows other pods or services to communicate with them

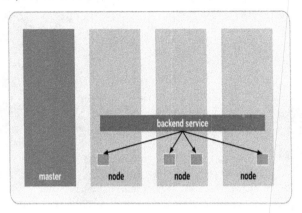

In Kubernetes, a service is an important component that acts a central internal load balancer and representatives of the pods. Services can also be defined as a long-lasting, well-known endpoint that points to a set of pods in a cluster. Services consist of three critical components: an external IP address (known as a portal, or sometimes a portal IP), a port and a label selector. Service is usually revealed through a small proxy process. The service proxy is responsible for deciding which pod to

148

route to an endpoint request via a label selector. It also acts as a thin look-up service to determine a way of handling the request. The service proxy is, therefore, in simple terms, a tuple that maps a portal, port, and label selector.

A service abstraction is essential to allow you to scale out or replace the backend work units as necessary. A service's IP address remains unchanged and stable regardless of the changes to the pods it routes too. When you deploy a service, you are simply gaining discoverability and can simplify your container designs. A service should be configured any time you need to provide access to one or more pods to another application or external consumers. For example, if you have a set of pods running web servers that should be accessible from the internet, a service will provide the necessary concept. Similarly, if a web service needs to store and recover data, an internal service is required to authorize access to the database pods.

In most circumstances, services are only

available via the use of an internally routable IP address. However, they can also be made available from their usual places through the use of several strategies, such as the NodePort configuration which works by opening a static port on each node's external networking interface. In this strategy, the traffic to the external port is routed automatically using an internal cluster IP service to the appropriate pods. Instead, the Load Balancer service strategy can be used to create an external load balancer which, in turn, routes to the services using a cloud provider's load balancer integration. The cloud controller manager, in turn, creates an appropriate resource and configures it using an internal service address. In summary, the main functionality of services in Kubernetes is to expose a pod's unique IP address which is usually not exposed outside the cluster without a service.

You can have multiple services with different configurations and features

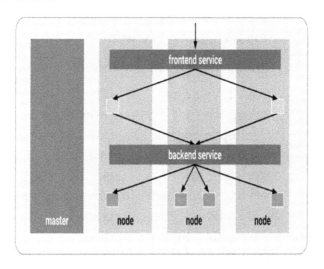

Service Discovery

Service discovery refers to the process of establishing how to connect to a service. Services need dynamically to discover each other to obtain IP addresses and port detail which are essential in communicating with other services in the cluster.Kubernetes offers two mechanisms of service discovery: DNS and environmental variable. While there is a service discovery option based on environmental variables available, most users prefer the DNS-based service discovery. Both are discussed below.

Service Discovery with

Environmental Variables

This mechanism of service discovery occurs when a pod exposes a service on a node, initiating Kubernetes to develop a set of environmental variables on the exposed node to describe the new service. This way, other pods on the same node can consume it easily. Managing service discovery using environmental variable mechanism is not scalable, therefore, most people prefer the Cluster DNS to discover services.

Cluster DNS

Cluster DNS enables a pod to discover services in the cluster, thereby enabling services to communicate with each other without having to worry about IP addresses and other fragile schemes. With cluster DNS, you can configure your cluster to schedule a pod and service that expose DNS. Then, when new pods are developed, they are informed of this service and will use it for look-ups. The cluster DNS is made of three special containers listed below:

- Etcd - Important for storing all the actual look-up information.

- SkyDns- It is a special DNS server written to read from etcd.

- Kube2sky - It is a Kubernetes-specific program that watches the master for any changes to the list of services and then publishes the information into etcd. SkyDns will then pick it up.

Apart from environmental variables and cluster DNS, there are other mechanisms which you can use to expose some of the services in your cluster to the rest of the world. This mechanism includes Direct Access, DIY Load Balancing, and Managed Hosting.

Direct Access- Involves configuring the firewall to pass traffic from the outside world to the portal IP of your service. Then, the proxy located on the node selects the container requested by the service. However, direct access faces a problem of limitation where you are constrained to only one pod to service the request, therefore, fault intolerant.

DIY Load Balancing- Involves placing the load balancer in front of the cluster and then populating it with the portal IPs of your service; therefore, you will have multiple pods available for the service request.

Managed Hosting- Most cloud providers supporting Kubernetes offer an easier way to make your services discoverable. All you need to do is to define your service by including a flag named *CreateExternalLoadBalncer* and set its value to *true*. By doing this, the cloud provider automatically adds the portal IPs for your service to a fleet of load balancers that is created on your behalf.

ReplicaSets-Replica Set Theory/Hands-on with ReplicaSets

As mentioned earlier, ReplicaSets is an advanced version of Replication Controller, offering greater flexibility in how the controller establishes the pods it is meant to manage. A ReplicaSet ensures that a specified number of pod replicas are running at any given time. Deployment can be used to effectively manage ReplicaSets as it enables it to provide declarative updates to pods combined with a lot of other useful features.

Using ReplicaSets is quite easy since most Kubernetes commands supporting Replication Controllers also support ReplicaSets except the rolling update command which is best used in Deployments. While ReplicaSets can be used independent of each other, it is best used by Deployments as a mechanism of orchestrating pod creation, deletion, and updates. By using

155

Deployments, you will not have to worry about managing the ReplicaSets they develop as they deploy and manage their ReplicaSets.

Daemon Sets

Daemon Sets are a specialized form of pod controller which runs a copy of a pod on each node in the cluster (or a subset, if specified). Daemon Sets are useful when deploying pods which help perform maintenance and provide services for the nodes themselves by creating pods on each added node, and garbage collects pods when nodes are removed from the cluster. Daemon Sets can be used for running daemons that require running on all nodes of a cluster. Such things can be cluster storage daemons, such as Qubyte, ceph, glusterd, etc., log collectors such as Fluentd or Logstash, or monitoring daemons such as Prometheus Node Exporter, Collectd, New Relic agent, etc.

The daemon can be deployed to all nodes, but it's important to split a single daemon to multiple daemons. Note that in situations involving a cluster with nodes of different hardware requiring adaption in the memory and CPU, you may have to include for the daemon for effective functionality.

There are other cases where you may require different logging, monitoring, or storage solutions on separate nodes of your cluster. In such circumstances where you prefer to deploy the daemons only to a specific set of nodes rather than the entire node, you may use a node selector to specify a subdivision of the nodes linked to the Daemon Set. For this to function effectively, you should have labeled your nodes consequently.

There are four main mechanisms in which you can communicate to the daemons discussed below:

- Push - In this mechanism, the pods are configured to push data to a service, making the services undiscoverable to clients.

- NodeIP and known port - The pods utilize a host port, enabling

157

clients to access each NodeIP via this port.

- DNS - In this mechanism, pods are accessed via a headless service by either the use of an endpoints resource or obtaining several A Records from DNS.

- Service - The pods are accessible via the standard service. The client can access a daemon on a random node using the same service; however, in this mechanism, you may not be able to access a specific node.

Since Daemon Sets are tasked to provide essential services and are required throughout the fleet, they, therefore, are allowed to bypass pod scheduling restrictions which limit other controllers from delegating pods to certain hosts. For instance, attributed to its unique responsibilities, the master server is usually configured to be inaccessible for normal pod scheduling, providing Daemon Sets with the ability to override the limitation on the pod-by-pod basis to ensure that essential services are running.

As per now, Kubernetes does not offer a mechanism of automatically updating a node. Therefore, you can only use the semi-automatic way of updating the pods by deleting the daemon set with the −cascade=false option, so that the pods may allot on the nodes; then you can develop a new Daemon Set with an identical pod selector and an updated pod template. The new Daemon Set will automatically recognize the previous pods, but will not automatically update them; however, you will need to use the new pod templates after manually deleting the previous pods from the nodes.

Jobs

Jobs are workloads used by Kubernetes to offer a more task-built workflow where the running containers are expected to exit successfully after completing the workload. Unlike the characteristic pod which is used to run long-running processes, jobs allow you to manage pods that are required to be terminated rather than being redeployed. A job can create one or more pods and guarantees the termination of a particular number of pods. Jobs can be used to achieve a typical batch-job such as backing up a database or deploying workers that need to function off a specific queue, i.e., image or video converters. There are various types of jobs as discussed below:

Non-parallel Jobs

In this type of job, one pod is usually initiated and goes on to complete the job after it has been terminated successfully. Incase of a failure in the pod, another one is created almost immediately to take its place.

Parallel Job with a fixed completion count

In a parallel job with a fixed completion count, a job is considered complete when there is one successful pod for every value between 1 and the number of completions specified.

Parallel Jobs with a work queue

With parallel jobs with a work queue, no pod is terminated lest the work queue is empty. This means that even if the worker performed its job, the pod could only be terminated successfully when the worker approves that all its fellow workers are also done. Consequently, all other pods are required to be terminated in the process of existing. Requested parallelism can be defined by parallel Jobs. For instance, if a job is set to 0, then the job is fundamentally paused until it is increased. It is worth noting that parallel jobs cannot support situations which require closely-communicating parallel processes, for example, in scientific computations.

CronJobs

CronJobs are used to schedule jobs or program the repetition of jobs at a specific point in time. They are analogous to jobs but with the addition of a schedule in Cron format.

ConfigMaps and Secrets

Kubernetes offers two separate storage locations for storing configuration information: Secrets for storing sensitive information and ConfigMaps for storing general configuration. Secrets and ConfigMaps are very similar in usage and support some use cases. ConfigMaps provides a mechanism of storing configuration in the environment rather than using code. It is important to store an application's configuration in the environment since an application can change configuration through development, staging, production, etc.; therefore, storing configuration in the environment increases portability of applications. ConfigMaps and Secrets are discussed below in detail.

Secrets

As mentioned above, Secrets are important for storing miniature amounts, i.e., less than I MB each of sensitive information such as keys, tokens, and passwords, etc. Kubernetes has a mechanism of creating and using Secrets automatically, for instance, Service Account token for accessing the API from a pod and it is also easy for users to create their passwords. It is quite simple to use passwords; you just have to reference them in a pod and then utilize them as either file at your own specified mount points, or as environmental variables in your pod. Note that each container in your pod is supposed to access the Secret needs to request it explicitly. However, there is no understood mechanism of sharing of Secrets inside the pod.

PullSecrets are a special type of Secret that can be used to bypass a Docker or another container image registry login to the Kubelet so that it can extract a private image for your pod. You need to be extremely cautious when updating Secrets that are in use by running pods since the pods in operation would not automatically pull the updated Secret. Additionally, you will need to explicitly update your pods, i.e., using the rolling update functionality of Deployments discussed above, or by restarting or recreating them. Put in mind that a Secret is namespaced, meaning that they are placed on a specific namespace, and only pods in the same namespace can access the Secret.

Secrets are stored in tmpfs and only stored on nodes that run pods which utilize those Secrets. The tmpfs keep Secrets from being accessible by the rest of the nodes in an application. Secrets are transmitted to and from the API server in plain text; therefore, you have to implement the SSL/TLS protected connections between user and API server and additionally between the API server and kubelets.

To enhance security for secrets, you should encrypt secrets in etcd. To add another layer of security, you should enable Node Authorization in Kubernetes, so that a kubelet can only request Secrets of Pods about its node. This function is to decrease the blast radius of a security breach on a node.

ConfigMaps

ConfigMaps are arguably similar to Secrets, only that they are designed to efficiently support working with strings that do not contain sensitive information. ConfigMaps can be used to store individual properties in the form of key-value pairs; however, the values can also be entirely used to configure files or JSON blobs to store more information. Configuration data can then be used to:

- Configure the environmental variable.

- Command-line arguments for a container.

- Configure files in a volume.

- Storing configuration files for tools like Redis or Prometheus which allows you to change the configuration of containers without having to rebuild the entire container.

ConfigMaps differs from Secrets in that it necessarily gets updated without the

165

need to restart the pods which use them. Nevertheless, depending on how to implement the configuration provided, you may need to reload the configs, e.g., using an API call to Prometheus to reload. This is often done through a sidecar container in the same pod watching for changes in the config file.

The most important thing about ConfigMaps and Secrets is that they function to enhance the versatility of containers by limiting their specificities which allow users to deploy them in different ways. Therefore, users are provided with a choice of reusing containers or among teams, or even outside the organization due to the elimination of container specificity. Secrets are especially helpful when sharing with other teams and organizations, or even when sharing publicly. This enables you to freely share images, for instance, via a public respiratory, without having to worry about any company-specific or sensitive data being published.

How is it going till now? Before moving to the deployment part just recap the topics you just went through. Also, can you spare some time and review the book?

3. Deployments

In Kubernetes, deployments are essential for deploying and managing software; therefore, it is important to comprehend how they function and how to use effectively. Before deployment, there were Replication Controllers, which managed pods and ensured a certain number of them were operating. With deployments, we moved to ReplicaSets, which replaced Replication Controllers later on. ReplicaSets are not usually managed; rather they get managed by Deployments we define through a definite chain, i.e., Deployment-ReplicaSet-Pod(s). In addition to what ReplicaSets offer, Deployment offers you declarative control over the update strategy used for the pods. This replaces the old kubectl rolling-update way of updating, but offers similar flexibility regarding defining maxSurge and maxUnavailable, i.e., how many additional and how many unavailable pods are allowed.

Deployments can manage your updates and even go as far as checking whether or not a new version being rolled out is working, and stop the rollout in case it is not. Additionally, you can indicate a wait time needed by a pod to be ready without any of its containers crashing before it's considered available, prevents "bad updates" giving your containers plenty of time to get ready to handle traffic. Furthermore, Deployments store a history of their revisions which can be used in rollback situations, as well as an event log, that can be used to audit releases and changes to your Deployment.

Integrating Storage Solutions and Kubernetes

Today, organizations are struggling to deliver solutions which will allow them to meet quickly changing business needs, as well as to address competitive pressure. To achieve this, they are utilizing various technologies such as containers, Kubernetes, and programmable infrastructure to achieve continuous integration/continuous development (CI/CD) and DevOps transformations.

For organizations deploying these technologies, they have to ensure tenacious storage across containers as it is important to maximize the number of applications in the model. One such example of an integrated storage solution which can be integrated to Kubernetes is NetApp Trident which is discussed in detail below.

NetApp Trident

Unlike competitive application container orchestration and dynamic storage provisioning plugins, NetApp Trident integrates with Kubernetes' persistent volume (PV) framework. Red Hat OpenShift with Trident provides one interface for dynamic provision of a persistent volume of applications across storage classes. These interfaces can be allocated to any of the storage platforms from NetApp to deliver the optimal storage management capabilities and performance for each application.

Trident was developed as an open source project by NetApp to offer Kubernetes users an external mechanism of monitoring Kubernetes volume and to completely automate the provisioning process. Trident can be integrated to Kubernetes and deployed as a physical server for storage, a virtual host, or a Kubernetes Pod. Trident offers Kubernetes a persistent storage solution and can be used in situations such as:

- In cloud-native applications and microservices.

- Traditional enterprise applications deployed in a hybrid cloud.

- DevOps teams who want to accelerate the CI/CD pipeline.

Trident also provides a boost of advanced features which are designed to offer deployment flexibility in

Kubernetes containerized applications, in addition to providing basic persistent volume integration. With Trident, you can:

- Configure storage via a simple Representational State Transfer application programming interface (REST API) with unique concepts that contain specific capabilities to Kubernetes storage classes.

- Protect and manage application data with NetApp enterprise-class storage. Current storage objects, such as volumes and logical unit numbers (LUNs), can easily be used by Trident.

- Based on your choice, you can use separate NetApp storage backends and deploy each with different configurations, thus allowing Trident to provide and consume storage with separate features, and present that storage to container-deployed workloads in a straightforward fashion.

Integrating the Trident dynamic storage provider to Kubernetes as a storage solution offers numerous benefits outlined below:

- Enables you to develop and deploy applications faster with rapid iterative testing.

- It provides a dynamic storage solution across storage classes of the entire storage portfolio of SolidFire, E-Series, NetApp, and ONTAP storage platforms.

- Improves efficiency when developing applications using Kubernetes.

Deploying Real World Application

To give you a better idea on how to deploy the real-world application, we are going to use a real-world application, i.e., Parse.

Parse

Parse is a cloud API designed to provide easy-to-use storage for mobile applications. It offers a variety of different client libraries making it easy to integrate with Android, iOS and other mobile platforms. Here is how you can deploy Parse in Kubernetes:

Fundamentals

Parse utilizes MongoDB cluster for its storage, therefore, you have to set up a replicated MongoDB using Kubernetes StatefulSets. Additionally, you should have a Kubernetes cluster deployed and ensure that the kubectl tool is properly configured.

Building the parse-server

The open source parse-server comes with a Dockerfile for easy containerization of the clone Parse repository.

```
$ git clone https://github.com/ParsePlatform/parse-server
```

Then move into that directory and build the image:

$ cd parse-server

$ docker build -t ${DOCKER_USER}/parse-server.

Finally, push that image up to the Docker hub:

$ docker push ${DOCKER_USER}/parse-server

Deploying the parse-server

Once a container image is developed, it is easy to deploy the parse-server into your cluster using the environmental variables configuration below:

APPLICATION-ID-An identifier for authorizing your application.

MASTER-KEY-An identifier that authorizes the master user.

DATABASE-URI-It is the URI for your MongoDB cluster.

When all these are placed together, it is

possible to deploy Parse as a Kubernetes Deployment using the YAML as illustrated below:

```
apiVersion: extensions/v1beta1
kind: Deployment
metadata:
  name: parse-server
  namespace: default
spec:
  replicas: 1
  template:
    metadata:
      labels:
        run: parse-server
    spec:
      containers:
      - name: parse-server
        image: ${DOCKER_USER}/parse-server
        env:
        - name: DATABASE_URI
          value: "mongodb://mongo-0.mongo:27017,\
            mongo-1.mongo:27017,mongo-2.mongo\
            :27017/dev?replicaSet=rs0"
        - name: APP_ID
          value: my-app-id
        - name: MASTER_KEY
          value: my-master-key
```

Testing Parse

It is important to test the deployment and this can be done by exposing it as a

176

Kubernetes service as illustrated below:

```
apiVersion: v1
kind: Service
metadata:
  name: parse-server
  namespace: default
spec:
  ports:
  - port: 1337
    protocol: TCP
    targetPort: 1337
  selector:
    run: parse-server
```

After testing confirms its operation, the parse then knows to receive a request from any mobile application; however, you should always remember to secure the connection with HTTPS after deploying it.

How to Perform a Rolling Update

A rolling update refers to the process of updating an application regarding its configuration or just when it is new. Updates are important as they keep applications up and running; however, it is impossible to update all features of an application all at once since the application will likely experience a downtime. Performing a rolling update is therefore important as it allows you to catch errors during the process so that you can rollback before it affects all of your users.

Rolling updates can be achieved through the use of Kubernetes Replication Controllers and the kubectl rolling-update command; however, in the latest version, i.e., Kubernetes 1.2, the Deployment object API was released in beta. Deployments function at a more advanced level as compared to Controllers and therefore are the preferred mechanism of performing rolling updates. First, let's look at how to complete a rolling update with a replication controller then later using Deployment API.

Rolling Updates with a Replication Controller

You will need a new a new Replication Controller with the updated configuration. The rolling update process synchronizes the rise of the replica count for the new Replication Controller, while lowering the number of replicas for the previous Replication Controller. This process lasts until the desired number of pods are operating with the new configuration defined in the new Replication Controller. After the process is completed, the old replication is then deleted from the system. Below is an illustration of updating a deployed application to a newer version using Replication Controller:

```
apiVersion: v1
kind: ReplicationController
metadata:
  name: k8s-deployment-demo-controller-v2
spec:
  replicas: 4
  selector:
    app: k8s-deployment-demo
    version: v0.2
  template:
    metadata:
      labels:
        app: k8s-deployment-demo
        version: v0.2
    spec:
      containers:
        - name: k8s-deployment-demo
          image: ryane/k8s-deployment-demo:0.2
          imagePullPolicy: Always
          ports:
            - containerPort: 8081
              protocol: TCP
          env:
            - name: DEMO_ENV
              value: production
```

To perform an update, kubectl rolling-update is used to stipulate that we want to update the running k8s-deployment-demo-controller-v1 Replication controller to k8-deployment-demo-controller-v2as illustrated below:

```
$ kubectl rolling-update k8s-deployment-demo-controller-v1 --updat
◄           III                              ►
```

180

Rolling updates with a Replication Controller faces some limitations, such that if you store your Kubernetes displays in source control, you may need to change at least two manifests to co-ordinate between releases. Additionally, the rolling update is more susceptible to network disruptions, coupled with the complexity of performing rollbacks, as it requires performing another rolling update back to another Replication Controller with an earlier configuration thereby lacking an audit trail. An easier method was developed to perform rolling updates with a deployment as discussed below:

Rolling Updates with a Deployment

Rolling updates with a deployment is quite simple, and similar rolling updates with Replication Control with a few differences are shown below:

```
apiVersion: extensions/v1beta1
kind: Deployment
metadata:
  name: k8s-deployment-demo-deployment
spec:
  replicas: 4
  selector:
    matchLabels:
      app: k8s-deployment-demo
  minReadySeconds: 10
  template:
    metadata:
      labels:
        app: k8s-deployment-demo
        version: v0.1
    spec:
      containers:
        - name: k8s-deployment-demo
          image: ryane/k8s-deployment-demo:0.1
          imagePullPolicy: Always
          ports:
            - containerPort: 8081
              protocol: TCP
          env:
            - name: DEMO_ENV
              value: staging
```

The differences are

- The selector uses match labels since the Deployment objects support set-based label requirements.

- The version label is excluded by the selector. The same deployment object supports multiple versions of the application.

The kubectl create function is used to run the deployment as illustrated below:

```
$ kubectl create -f demo-deployment-v1.yml --record
deployment "k8s-deployment-demo-deployment" created
```

This function saves the command together with the resource located in the Kubernetes API server. When using a deployment, four pods run the application to create the Deployment objects as shown below:

As mentioned earlier on, one advantage of using deployment is that the update history is always stored in Kubernetes and the kubectl rollout command can be

```
$ kubectl get pods
NAME                                                 READY   STATUS
k8s-deployment-demo-deployment-3774590724-2scro      1/1     Runnir
k8s-deployment-demo-deployment-3774590724-cdtsh      1/1     Runnir
k8s-deployment-demo-deployment-3774590724-dokm9      1/1     Runnir
k8s-deployment-demo-deployment-3774590724-m58pe      1/1     Runnir

$ kubectl get deployment
NAME                             DESIRED   CURRENT   UP-TO-DATE
k8s-deployment-demo-deployment   4         4         4
```

used to view the update history illustrated below:

```
$ kubectl rollout history deployment k8s-deployment-demo-deployment
deployments "k8s-deployment-demo-deployment":
REVISION        CHANGE-CAUSE
1               kubectl create -f demo-deployment-v1.yml --record
2               kubectl apply -f demo-deployment-v2.yml --record
```

In conclusion, rolling updates is an essential feature in Kubernetes, and its efficiency is improved with each released version. The new Deployment feature in Kubernetes 1.2 provides a well-designed mechanism of managing application deployment.

Statefulness: Deploying Replicated Stateful Applications

Statefulness is essential in the case of the following application needs:

- Stable, persistent storage.

- Stable, unique network

identifiers.

- Ordered, automated rolling updates.

- Ordered, graceful deletion and termination.

- Ordered, graceful deployment and scaling.

In the above set of conditions, synonymous refers to tenacity across pod (re)scheduling.

Statefulness can be used instead of using ReplicaSet to operate and provide a stable identity for each pod. StatefulSet resources are personalized to applications where instances of the application must be treated as non-fungible individuals, with each having a stable name and state. A StatefulSet ensures that those pods are rescheduled in such a way that they maintain their identity and state. Additionally, it allows one to easily and efficiently scale the number of pets up and down. Just like ReplicaSets, StatefulSet has an anticipated replica count field which determines the number of pets you want operating at a given time. StatefulSet created pods from pod templates specific to the parts of the StatefulSet; however, unlike pods developed by ReplicaSets, pods created by the StatefulSet are not identical to each other. Each pod has its own set of volumes, i.e., storage, which differentiates it from its peers. Pet pods have a foreseeable and stable identity as opposed to new pods which gets a completely random number.

Every pod created by StatefulSet is allocated a zero index, which is then utilized to acquire the pod's name and hostname and to ascribe stable storage to the pod; therefore, the names of the pods are predictable since each pod's name is retrieved from the StatefulSet's name and the original index of the instance. The pods are well organized rather than being given random names.

In some situations, unlike regular pods, Stateful pods require to be addressable by their hostname, but this is not the case with regular pods.

Attributed to this, StatefulSet needs you to develop a corresponding governing headless service that is used to offer the actual network distinctiveness to each pod. In this service, each pod, therefore, gets its unique DNS entry; thus, its aristocracies and perhaps other clients in the network can address the pod by its hostname.

Deploying a Replicated Stateful Application

To deploy an app through StatefulSet, you will first need to create two or more separate types of objects outlined below:

- The StatefulSet itself.

- The governing service required by the StatefulSet.

- PersistentVolume for storing the data files.

The StatefulSet is programmed to develop a PersistantVolumeClaim for

187

every pod instance which will then bind to a persistent volume; however, if your cluster does not support dynamic provisioning, you will need to manually create PersistentVolume using the requirements outlined above.

To create the PersistentVolume required to scale the StatefulSet to more than tree replicas, you will first need to develop an authentic GCE Persistent Disks like the one illustrated below:

```
$ gcloud compute disks create --size=1GiB --zone=europe-west1-b pv-a
$ gcloud compute disks create --size=1GiB --zone=europe-west1-b pv-b
$ gcloud compute disks create --size=1GiB --zone=europe-west1-b pv-c
```

The GCE Persistent Storage Disk is used as the fundamental storage mechanism in Google's Kubernetes Engine.

The next step in deploying a replicated Stateful application is to create a governing service which is essential to provide the Stateful pods with a network identity. The governing service should contain:

- Name of the Service.

- The StatefulSet's governing service which should be headless.

- Pods which should be allotted labels synonymous to the service, i.e., app=kubia label.

After completing this step, you can then create the StatefulSet manifest as listed below:

```
apiVersion: apps/v1beta1
kind: StatefulSet
metadata:
  name: kubia
spec:
  serviceName: kubia
  replicas: 2
  template:
    metadata:
      labels:                              1
        app: kubia                         1
    spec:
      containers:
      - name: kubia
        image: luksa/kubia-pet
        ports:
        - name: http
          containerPort: 8080
        volumeMounts:
        - name: data                       2
          mountPath: /var/data             2
  volumeClaimTemplates:
  - metadata:                              3
      name: data                           3
    spec:                                  3
      resources:                           3
        requests:                          3
          storage: 1Mi                     3
      accessModes:                         3
      - ReadWriteOnce                      3
```

Later on, create the StatefulSet and a list of pods. The final product is that the StatefulSet will be configured to develop two replicas and will build a single pod. The second pod is then created after the first pod has started operating.

Understanding Kubernetes Internals

To understand Kubernetes internals, let's first discuss the two major divisions of the Kubernetes cluster:

- The Kubernetes Control Plane

- Nodes

- Add-on Components

The Kubernetes Control Panel

The control panel is responsible for overseeing the functions of the cluster. The components of the control panel include:

- The etcd distributed persistent storage

- The Controller Manager

- The Scheduler

- The API server

The components function is in unison to store and manage the state of the

191

cluster.

Nodes

The nodes function to run the containers and have the following components:

- The Kubelet

- The Container Runtime (Docker, rkt, or others)

- The Kubernetes Service Proxy (kube-proxy)

Add-on Components

Apart from the nodes and control panel, other components are required for Kubernetes to operate effectively. This includes:

- An Ingress controller

- The Dashboard

- The Kubernetes DNS server

- Heapster

- The Container Network Interface network plugin

192

Functioning of the Components

All the components outlined above interdepend among each other to function effectively; however, some components can carry out some operations independently without the other components. The components only communicate with the API server and not to each other directly. The only component that communicates with the etcd is the API server. Rather than the other components communicating directly with the etcd, they amend the cluster state by interacting with the API server. The system components always initiate the integration between the API server and other components. However, when using the command kubectl to retrieve system logs, the API server does not connect to the Kubelet and you will need to use kubectlattachorkubectl port-forward to connect to an operating container.

The components of the worker nodes can be distributed across multiple servers, despite components placed on the worker nodes operating on the same node. Additionally, only a single instance of a Scheduler and Controller Manager can be active at a time in spite of multiple instances of etcd and the API server being active concurrently performing their tasks in parallel.

The Control Plane components, along with the kube-proxy, run by either being deployed on the system directly or as pods. The Kubelet operates other components, such as pods, in addition to being the only components which operate as a regular system component. The Kubelet is always deployed on the master, to operate the Control Plane components as pods.

Kubernetes using etcd

Kubernetes uses etcd which is a distributed, fast, and reliable key-value store to prevent the API servers from failing and restarting due to the operating pressure experienced by storing the other components. As previously mentioned, Kubernetes is the only system component which directly communicates to etcd, thereby has a few benefits which include enhancing the optimistic locking system coupled with validation, and providing the only storage location for storing cluster state and metadata.

Function Of The Api Server

In Kubernetes, the API server is the primary component used by another system component as well as clients such as kubectl. The API server offers a CRUD (Create, Read, Update, and Delete) interface, which is important for querying and modifying the cluster state over a RESTful API in addition to storing the state in etcd. The API server is also a validation of objects to prevent clients from storing improperly constructed objects. Additionally, it also performs optimistic locking, therefore, variations in an object are never superseded by other clients in the situation of concurrent updates.

It is important to note that the API server does not perform any other task away from what is discussed above. For instance, it does not create pods when you develop a ReplicaSet resource, nor does it overlook the endpoints of a service. Additionally, the API server is not responsible for directing controllers to perform their task; rather, it allows controllers and other system components to monitor changes to deployed resources.

kubectlis an example of an API server's client tool and is essential for supporting watching resources. For instance, when deploying a pod, you don't have to continuously poll the list of pods by repeatedly executing kubectl get pods.

Rather, you may use the watchflag to be notified of each development, modification, or deletion of a pod.

The Function of Kubelet

In summary, Kubelet is in charge of every operation on a worker node. Its main task is to register the node it is operating by creating a node resource in the API server. Also, it needs to constantly oversee the API server for pods that have been scheduled to the
196

node, and the start of the pod's container. Additionally, it continuously monitors running containers and informs the API server of their resource consumption, status, and events.

The other functionality of Kubelet is to run the container liveness probes and restarting containers following the failure of probes, in addition to terminating containers when their pod is deleted from the API server and notifies the server that the pod has been terminated.

Securing the Kubernetes API Server

Think of this situation; you have an operational Kubernetes cluster which is functioning on a non-secure port accessible to anyone in the organization. This is extremely dangerous as data in the API server is exceptionally susceptible to breaches; therefore, you have to secure the API server to maintain data integrity. To secure the API server, you must first retrieve the server and client certificates by using a token to stipulate a service account, and then you configure the API server to find a secure port and update the Kubernetes master and node configurations. Here is a detailed explanation:

Transport Security

The API server usually presents a self-signed certificate on the user's machine in this format: $USER/. kube/config. The API server's certificate is usually contained in the root certificate which, when specified, can be used in the place of the system default root certificate. The root certificate is automatically placed in $USER/. kube/config upon creating a cluster using kube-up.sh

Authentication

The authentication step is next after a TLS is confirmed. In this step, the cluster creation script or cluster admin configure the API server to operate one or more Authenticator Modules made up of key components, including Client Certificate, Password, Bootstrap Tokens, Plain Tokens and JWT Tokens. Several authentication modules can be stated after trial and error until the perfect match succeeds. However, if the request cannot be authenticated, it is automatically rejected with HTTP status code 401. In the case of authentication, the user is provided with a specific username which can be used in subsequent steps. Authenticators vary widely with others providing usernames for group members, while others decline them altogether. Kubernetes uses usernames for access control decisions and in request logging.

Authorization

The next step is the authorization of an authenticated request from a specified user. The request should include the username of a requester, the requested action, and the object to be initiated by request. The request is only authorized by an available policy affirming that the user has been granted the approval to accomplish the requested action.

With Kubernetes authorization, the user is mandated to use common REST

199

attributes to interact with existing organization-wide or cloud-provider-wide access control systems. Kubernetes is compatible with various multiple authorization modules such as ABAC mode, RBAC Mode, and Webhook mode.

Admission Control

This is a software module that functions to reject or modify user requests. These modules can access the object's contents which are being created or updated. They function on objects being created, deleted, updated or connected. It is possible to configure various admission controllers to each other through an order. Contrary to Authentication and Authorization Modules, the Admission Control Module can reject a request leading to the termination of the entire request. However, once a request has been accepted by all the admission controllers' modules, then it is validated via the conforming API object, and then written to the object store.

Securing Cluster Nodes and Networks

In addition to securing a Kubernetes API server, it is also extremely important to secure cluster nodes and networks as it is the first line of defense to limit and control users who can access the cluster and the actions they are allowed to perform. Securing cluster nodes and networks involves various dimensions which are listed below and are later discussed in detail:

- Controlling access to the Kubernetes API

- Controlling access to the Kubelet

- Controlling the capabilities of a workload or user at runtime

- Protecting cluster components from compromise

Controlling Access to the Kubernetes API

The central functionality of Kubernetes

lies with the API, therefore, should be the first component to be secured. Access to the Kubernetes API can be achieved through: Using Transport Level Security (TLS) for all API traffic - It a requirement by Kubernetes that all API communication should be encrypted by default with TLS, and the majority of the installation mechanism should allow the required certificates to be developed and distributed to the cluster component.

API Authentication - The user should choose the most appropriate mechanism of authentication, such that the accessed pattern used should match those used in the cluster node. Additionally, all clients must be authenticated, including those who are part of the infrastructure like nodes, proxies, the scheduler and volume plugins.

API Authorization - Authorization happens after authentication, and every request should pass an authorization check. Broad and straightforward roles may be appropriate for smaller clusters

202

and may be necessary to separate teams into separate namespaces when more users interact with the cluster.

Controlling access to the Kubelet

Believe it or not, Kubelets allow unauthenticated access to the API server as it exposes HTTPS endpoints, thereby providing a strong control over the node and containers. However, production clusters, when used effectively, enable Kubelet to authorize and authenticate requests thus securing cluster nodes and networks

Controlling the capabilities of a workload or user at runtime

Controlling the capabilities of a workload can secure cluster nodes by ensuring high-level authorization in Kubernetes. This can be done through:

- Limiting resource usage on a cluster

- Controlling which privileges containers run with

- Restricting network access

- Restricting cloud metadata API access

- Controlling which nodes Pods may access

Protecting cluster components from compromise

By protecting cluster components from compromise, you can secure cluster nodes and networks by:

- Restricting access to etcd

- Enable audit logging

- Restricting access to alpha and beta features

- Reviewing third-party integrations before enabling them

- Encrypting secrets at rest

- Receiving security alert updates and reporting vulnerabilities

Managing Pods Computational Resources

When creating pods, it is important to consider how much CPU and computer memory a pod is likely to consume, and the maximum amount it is required to consume. This ensures that a pod is only allocated the required resources by the Kubernetes cluster, in addition to determining how they will be scheduled across the cluster. When developing pods, it is possible to indicate how much CPU and memory each container requires. After the specifications have been indicated, the scheduler then decides on how to allocate each pod to a node.

Each container of a pod can specify the required resources as shown below:

- `spec.containers[].resources.limits.cpu`

- `spec.containers[].resources.limits.memory`

- `spec.containers[].resources.requests.cpu`

- `spec.containers[].resources.requests.memory`

While computational resources requests and limits can only be specified to individual containers, it is essential to indicate pod resource and request as well. A pod resource limit stipulates the amount of resource required for each container in the pod.

When a pod is created, the Kubernetes scheduler picks a node in which the pod will operate on. Each node has a maximum limit for each of the resource type, i.e., the memory and CPU. The scheduler is tasked to ensure that the amount of each requested resource of the scheduled containers should always be less than the capacity of the node. The scheduler is highly effective that it declines to place a pod on a node if the actual CPU or memory usage is extremely low and that the capacity check has failed. This is important to guard against a shortage in the resource on a node incase of an increase in resource usage later, for instance, during a period peak in the service request rate.

Running OF PODS with Resource limits

When a container of a pod is started by Kubelet, it passes the CPU and memory limits to the container runtime as a confirmatory test. In this test, if a container surpasses the set memory limit, it might be terminated. However, if it is restartable, the Kubelet will restart it, together with any form of runtime failure. In the case that a container exceeds its memory specifications, the pod will likely be evicted every time the node's available memory is exhausted. A container is not allowed to outdo its CPU limit for extended periods of time, although it will not be terminated for excessive CPU usage.

Automatic scaling of pods and cluster nodes

Pods and cluster nodes can be manually scaled, mostly in the case of expected load spikes in advance, or when the load changes gradually over a longer period, requiring manual intervention to manage a sudden, unpredictable increase in traffic or service request. Manual scaling is not efficient and it is ideal, therefore, that Kubernetes provides an automatic mechanism to monitor pods and automatically scale them up in situations of increased CPU usage attributed to an increase in traffic.

The process of autoscaling pods and cluster nodes is divided into three main steps:

- Acquiring metrics off all the pods that are managed by the scaled resource object.

- Calculating the number of pods required to maintain the metrics at the specified target value.

- Update the replicas field of the scaled resource.

The process commences with the horizontal pod autoscaler controller, obtaining the metrics of all the pods by querying Heapster through REST calls. The Heapster should be running in the cluster for autoscaling to function once the Autoscaler obtains the metrics for the pod belonging to the system component in a question of being scaled. The Autoscaler then uses the obtained metrics to determine the number that will lower the average value of the metric across all the replicas as close as possible. This is done by adding the metric values obtained from all the pods and dividing the value by the target value set on the HorizontalPodAutoscaler resource and then rounding the value to the next larger value. The final step of autoscaling is updating the anticipated replica count field on the scaled component and then allowing the

Replica-Set controller to spin up additional pods or delete the ones in excess altogether.

Extending Kubernetes Advanced Scheduling

Kubernetes has an attribute of being an advanced scheduler; therefore, it provides a variety of options to users to stipulate conditions for allocating pods to particular nodes that meet a certain condition, rather than basing it on available resources of the node. Kubernetes advanced scheduling is achieved through the master API which is a component that provides offers to read/write access to the cluster's desired and current state. The scheduler uses the master API to retrieve existing information, carry out some calculations and then update the API with new information relating to the desired state.

Kubernetes utilizes controller patterns to uphold and update the cluster state where the scheduler controller is particularly responsible for pod-scheduling decisions. The scheduler constantly monitors the Kubernetes API to find unscheduled pods and decides on which node the pods will be placed on. The decision to create a new pod by the scheduler is achieved after three stages:

- Node filtering

- Node priority calculation

- Actual scheduling operation

In the first stage, the scheduler identifies a node which is compatible with the running workload. A compatible node is identified by passing all nodes via a set of filters and eliminating those which are not compatible with the required configurations. The following filters are used:

- Volume filters

- Resource filters

- Affinity selectors

In addition to scheduling, cluster users and administrators can update the

211

cluster state by viewing it via the Kubernetes dashboard which enables them to access the API.

Best Practices for Developing Apps

After going through much of the content in developing applications with Kubernetes, here are some of the tips for creating, deploying and running applications on Kubernetes.

Building Containers

- Keep base images small - It is an important practice to start building containers from the smallest viable image and then advancing with bigger packages as you continue with the development. Smaller base images have some advantages including it builds faster, it has less storage, it is less likely to attack surface and occupies less storage.

- Don't trust just any base image -

Most people would just take a created image from DockerHub, and this is dangerous. For instance, you may be using a wrong version of the code, or the image could have a bug in it, or, even worse, it could be a malware. Always ensure that you use your base image.

Container Internals

- Always use a non-root user inside the container - A non-root user is important in the situation that someone hacks into your container and you haven't changed the user from a root. In this situation, the hacker can access the host via a simple container escape but, on changing the user to non-root, the hacker will need numerous hack attempts to gain root access.

- Ensure one process per container - It is possible to run more than one process in a container; however, it is advised to run only a single process since Kubernetes manages containers based on their health.

Deployments

- Use plenty of descriptive labels when deploying - Labels are arbitrary key-value pairs, therefore, are very powerful deployment tools.

- Use sidecars for Proxies, watchers, etc. - A group of processes may be needed to communicate with one another, but they should not run on a single container.

How to Deploy Applications That Have Pods with Persistent Dependencies

You can have applications having persistent pod dependencies using the Blue-Green Deployment mechanism. This mechanism involves operating two versions of an application concurrently, and moving production traffic between the old and new version. The Blue-Green deployment mechanism switches between two different versions of an application which support N-1 compatibility. The old and new versions of the application are used to distinguish between the two apps.

How to Handle Back-Up and Recovery of Persistent Storage In The Context Of Kubernetes

Persistent storage in Kubernetes can be handled with etcd which is a consistent and an essential key-value store since it acts as a storage location for all Kubernetes' cluster data. They ensure the correct functioning of etcd, and the following requirements are needed:

- Check out for resource starvation

- Run etcd as a cluster of odd members

- Ensure that the etcd leader timely relays heartbeats to followers to keep the followers stable

To ensure a smooth back-up, you may operate etcd with limited resources. Persistent storage problems can be eliminated by periodically backing up the cluster data which is essential in recovering the clusters in the case of losing master nodes. The Kubernetes states any critical information, i.e., secrets are contained in the snapshot file which can be encrypted to prevent unauthorized entry. Backing up Kubernetes clusters into the etcd cluster can be accomplished in two major ways: built-in snapshot and volume snapshot.

etcd clusters can be restored from snapshots which are taken and obtained from an etcd process of the major and minor version. etcd also supports the restoration of clusters with different patch versions. A restore operation is usually employed to recover the data of a failed cluster.

In the case of failure in the majority of etcd members, the etcd cluster is considered failed and therefore

Kubernetes cannot make any changes to its current state. In this case, the user can recover the etcd cluster and potentially reconfigure the Kubernetes API server to fix the issue.

How to Deploy An Application With Geographic Redundancy In Mind

Geo-Redundant applications can be deployed using Kubernetes via a linked pair of SDN-C. This is still a new concept developed in ONAP Beijing and involves using one site as an active site and the other site acting as a warm standby, which could also be used as an active site. The operator is tasked to monitor the health of the active site by establishing failures and initiating a scripted failover. They are also responsible for updating the DNS server so that the clients would direct their messaging towards the now-active site. A PROM component, which was added later on, can automatically update the DNS server and monitor health, thereby eliminating the need of having an operator. PROM relays the status of the site health and can make informed decisions.

4. Conclusion

In conclusion, while this guide offers you a good understanding of the essential components of Kubernetes, you have to carry out practical examples to gain a deeper understanding of the concepts. This guide only explains the basic functionalities, but does delve deeper into fundamental concepts. It is important to note that Kubernetes is a sophisticated resource for creating and deploying; therefore, you need to start with the basics as you go deeper into key functionalities. We hope this guide has been key in understanding the basic concepts of Kubernetes which are still a developing concept. Thank you

** How did you like the book? Could you spare some time and review it.

My Other Books available across the platforms in e-book, paperback and audible versions:

1. **Blockchain Technology : Introduction to Blockchain Technology and its impact on Business Ecosystem**

2. DevOps Handbook: Introduction to DevOps and its Impact on Business Ecosystem

3. Blockchain Technology and DevOps : Introduction and Impact on Business Ecosystem

4. Love Yourself: 21 day plan for learning "Self-Love" to cultivate self-worth ,self-belief, self-confidence & happiness

5. Intermittent Fasting: 7 effective techniques of Intermittent Fasting

7 EFFECTIVE TECHNIQUES OF

INTERMITTENT FASTING

Stay Healthy, Lose Weight,
Slow Down Aging Process & Live Longer!

STEPHEN FLEMING

6. Love Yourself and intermittent Fasting(Mind and Body Bundle Book)

You can check all my Books on my **Amazon's Author Page**

** If you prefer audible versions of these books, I have few free coupons, mail me at valueadd2life@gmail.com. If available, I would mail you the same.

www.ingramcontent.com/pod-product-compliance
Lightning Source LLC
Chambersburg PA
CBHW071241050326
40690CB00011B/2218